THE
JEET KUNE DO
MINDSET

Martial Arts Ways for a Better Life

Martin O'Neill

Let's Tell Your Story Publishing
London

COPYRIGHT

Title: The Jeet Kune Do Mindset: Martial Arts Ways for a Better Life

First published in 2017

Address 3 Century Court, Tolpits Lane, Watford, UK WD18 9RS

ISBN 9781910600146

Book design: Colette Mason

Editing: Greg Fidgeon

COPYRIGHT ACKNOWLEDGEMENTS

DISCLAIMER

"Life can only be understood backward; but it must be lived forward" – Kierkegaard

CONTENTS

ACKNOWLEDGEMENTS

I am very grateful to the following people. First to my wife Bernadette, who has more love, bravery and courage than I will ever have. Much love to Sorcha and Meabh, my beautiful daughters. My parents Rita and Joe, now deceased but always in our hearts. My smart and insightful book coach Colette Mason and my editor Greg Fidgeon.

My instructors Guro Dan Inosanto and Sigung Taky and Andy Kimura, Alain de Preter. Thanks to Guro "Cookie" Vassiliou and Simo Paula Inosanto. My senior students Johnny Bell, Barry Bell, Justin Weir, James Devine, Graham Cullen, Olivia Beattie, Jordan Weir. To Jimmy Hughes, Niall Hughes, Seamus McCooey, Peter Murtagh, Joshua Weir. The students who posed for photos: Andre Farell, Mark Maxwell, and John Brangan. Instructors Patrick van Vlasselaer, Rick Young, Daniel Lonero and Marie Sia, Joel Clark, Lamar Davis II, Peter Lavery and Jason Boh, Brian McCarthy.

Michael Campbell Photography, The Mall, Armagh, Peadar McConville Video Me Productions

My friends who keep my feet on the ground. All at Clann Eireann Youth Club, who have kept faith in young people during the nightmare that took place in Northern Ireland for 40 years.

Go raibh mile maith agaibh.

FOREWORD

Martin O'Neill has a scintillating personality. He never fails to keep you in stitches with deep laughter with his unique philosophy on life.

Behind this light-heartedness there glows a serious and thoughtful man who commands a high degree of respect. He has paid his dues and carried himself up by his bootstraps to deserve great respect and admiration from his peers.

In my judgement, his respect and deep feelings with regard to the inimitable teachings of Bruce Lee are rock solid and I know that there are martial artists, scholars and just plain folks who would wholeheartedly agree from the core of their hearts.

Martin has a very respectful martial arts background that precedes his exploration of Bruce Lee's art.

He is an excellent exponent of Bruce Lee's teaching. He is able to impart not only the physical but the philosophical message as well.

I know that Bruce would have welcomed Martin's sincerity.

The message at Bruce's grave site reads, "The key to immortality is to first live a life worth remembering." This resonates deeply with Sifu O'Neill and it is reflected in his actions.

Martin is a very sincere and compassionate warrior who understands the how and what to teach, and identifies with his students who come to him for physical and mental betterment, which ultimately advances to each and all to cope with the complexities of our being.

Martin, please "walk on" and continue to teach from the depths of your heart the true and inimitable teachings of our great leader, Bruce Lee.

Taky Kimura, Seattle, USA, 2008

Bruce Lee's Assistant Instructor

INTRODUCTION

ABOUT ME

Hi, I am Martin O'Neill. I was raised in a Northern Ireland "ghetto" during what is called "the Troubles" by the mass media. In reality, it was a civil war – thousands of people were killed and injured over a period of 40 years. The violence has generally ended but the resentment, hurt and hate bubbles away just under the surface.

I left school aged 15 feeling a complete failure and two years later found myself making trash cans. I later worked for many years as a welder across Ireland and in London.

By chance I discovered the Open University in my early 20s and enrolled on a social science foundation course. I couldn't make it to many of the tutorials due to having no transport. There was no bus home and it was too dangerous to hitch a ride at the time – people were being murdered all over the place. Somehow I still got through the first-year course.

I moved to London to join my girlfriend and started work as a welder while volunteering with homeless people at Centrepoint Soho. I was later accepted onto a four-year BA Hons social science and social work course as a mature student. For the next 30 years my career was in social work; spanning probation work, child care, disability, mental health, adult care and I ended up specialising in community development and social work.

I began training in martial arts in January 1976 in the karate style of Wado Ryu in Dublin, Ireland. This was at the height of the international Bruce Lee craze following his record-breaking movie, Enter the Dragon. I gained a 1st Dan black belt in 1980 and was involved in fighting in many semi and full contact bouts and tournaments.

In 1986, I enrolled as an apprentice instructor for five years with Steve and Mike Krause, who were instructors under Guro Dan Inosanto. In the early 1990s, I travelled to America and trained with Sifu Lamar M Davis II, who is a well known instructor in JKD. I studied with Lamar for nearly ten years becoming a full instructor in 2002.

Since 2000, I have been studying with the Jun Fan Gung Fu Institute in Seattle, USA, with Sigung Taky Kimura, his son Andy Kimura and my Sifu and dear friend Alain de Preter.

In 2008, I had a heart attack during a mass attack training session and almost died. I had to have an immediate triple bypass operation and it took more than a year for me to recover my strength to be able to return to training. I had to learn that my training needed to change as a result of the problem, but it was fantastic to be doing it again.

Then in 2013 I was delighted and humbled to be accepted as a student on the International Instructor Programme at the Inosanto Academy, USA – to train under the guidance of the brilliant Guro Dan Inosanto.

This has opened a new perspective on martial arts and life for me, highlighting the genius of the man and his incredible, generous teaching methodology.

I got into fights in my younger days, when I was an angry young man. I have been stabbed, bottled, punched, kicked, concussed, given black eyes and have had my feelings hurt along the way. Numerous brain cells have somehow disappeared into the ether.

However, I have lived to tell the tale and some of my stories are in this book along with advice on good training methods, defence techniques and how not to get battered. It also offers tips on improving your health and wellbeing, and how to live a more fulfilling lifestyle.

I have taught martial arts for 30 years at Clann Eireann Youth Club in Lurgan, County Armagh, which has been a very violent part of Northern Ireland; deeply affected by the Troubles.

Our JKD students are from many nationalities and different sections of the community. We have an open-door, inclusive, anti-sectarian, anti-racist approach – something that gives me pride.

"Under the stars under the heavens there is but one family"
Bruce Lee

WHO THIS BOOK IS FOR

This book is aimed at those who want to improve their lifestyle by taking a more thoughtful and considered approach to society and how it acts, while embracing the martial art of Jeet Kune Do (JKD).

You do not need to be currently practicing JKD and this is not intended to be a manual for experts: there are many technical books and resources available.

Instead, the book offers sound and solid information to those who want to make positive changes and includes advice on auditing your lifestyle, health and wellbeing, improving friendships, fitness, strength and analysing your current and future priorities.

The book also shares self-protection and personal defence techniques used in JKD that work in real world scenarios with practical advice on how to "clobber and overwhelm enemies " by using superior training and tactics to outwit them.

This approach is introduced and supported throughout the book. The JKD training methods will help you to have the confidence and competence to use your full abilities to succeed in life.

Surprisingly or not, our biggest enemy is often just ourselves and our over inflated egos.

"The price of wisdom is above rubies"
Job

A SHORT HISTORY OF JEET KUNE DO (JKD)

Who is Bruce Lee?

To many Bruce Lee was the most electrifying, innovative and inspiring martial arts movie star of the 20th century. He is also known as someone who died before his time, at the age of just 32.

However, when we look more closely we find a renaissance man, someone of great creativity, a philosophical thinker, writer, researcher, and family man. He was a fanatical physical trainer who changed his physique and athleticism beyond normal human boundaries.

His martial arts exploits are legend and he eventually created his own art of Jeet Kune Do (the way of the intercepting fist) dedicated to the creative martial artist.

Bruce was a phenomenon filled with boundless energy and creativity. He overcame obstacles in life that would have crushed most people. He remained a brave compassionate warrior for all his short life and worked against racism and discrimination. He encouraged and educated his students and fans to raise their horizons, smashing beyond the purely physical realm and make their dreams a reality and live each day to the full.

JKD therefore is a relatively young martial art, based on physics, physiology, kinesiology and psychology. It was created by Bruce in the early 1960s and it was further researched, developed and perpetuated by Guro Dan Inosanto. Sigung Taky and Andy Kimura are the keepers of the flame and guardians of Bruce's grave in Seattle, USA.

Bruce had trained in Wing Chun for several years in the 1950s under Grandmaster Ip Man in Hong Kong. But he was critical of some traditional martial ways, which seemed to hold the practitioner in set patterns that he called "organised despair".

Instead, he wanted a modern, scientific approach to test and evaluate the principles of combat and JKD against a resisting opponent. He advocated applying a rational manner to a training programme to ensure that it's straightforward, direct and effective, and honest.

Jeet Kune Do has its own ideas, philosophy and training methods that make it a unique martial art.

Begin training with Jun Fan Gung Fu (Bruce Lee's Gung Fu) ™

It's highly recommended to begin training with Jun Fan Gung Fu (JFGF) ™ as a base system, which has a curriculum. Some of this is outlined in this book. However, unlike Jun Fan Gung Fu and most martial arts, JKD does not have a set syllabus to follow. That's why it's important to have a solid foundation to build upon.

The technical basis of the art is:

- the on guard stance
- footwork and mobility
- punching and kicking
- five ways of attack
- economy of motion and interception
- energy sensitivity drills
- fighting skills in all ranges, standing and on the ground

Training methods are based on effectiveness, efficiency, practical application, and reality. Basic techniques need to be learned quickly and remembered easily to be effective. Street survival, and living a happy fruitful life through confidence, skill, creativity and love is the ultimate goal of the JKD practitioner.

Ironically, top practitioners are very humble and would never seek out trouble. However they would face up to a bully, mugger or tyrant in an instant; never backing down.

WHAT THIS BOOK COVERS

THE MINDSET OF JKD

There is more to JKD than the physical elements of combat. We will first look the mental aspects and other ways in which this martial art can have a massive impact on your life and how you live it.

We will discuss the ability to identify fear in a disciplined way and how failure to control this emotion can lead to disaster.

The JKD approach begins with self-help; building your confidence and self-esteem through participation in challenging training sessions that builds a fighting spirit and strong mind and body.

Only when this is done successfully do we advocate helping others to set and reach their goals, but examples are included of how to assist others and the pros and cons involved.

Giving something back to our friends and families and community is important in JKD. This goes way beyond the physical approach of being fit and tough. It goes into building a strong sense of self-worth, team spirit, leadership and paying back our instructors and being grateful to the creator.

The results of this can be as straightforward as listening to a person who is having a difficult time emotionally. It can give a sense of hope and fulfilment to young people seeking a positive role model, helping them to deal with risk taking behaviour due to substance misuse, for example.

The benefits of this section are about self-knowledge and giving back and being grateful to our loved ones and others.

JKD TRAINING AND EQUIPMENT

The most important pieces of equipment at your disposal are your mind and body. You will always need these and they will need to be kept in good condition to be effective.

This section will give a brief look into that as well as introducing other equipment such as boxing gloves, focus pads, skipping rope and heavy bag. But remember: you don't need a huge amount of equipment to get started.

INTRODUCTION TO THE WORKOUTS

You will be taken through a practical and challenging and progressive series of activities and training over a 12-week period.

The idea of this programme is to give you the best start in your training and take you to the next level of fitness and conditioning. The benefits of these activities are tried and tested, and will get you into great shape and improve your cardiovascular capacity and fitness.

FUNDAMENTAL TECHNIQUES OF JKD

You will be taught the fundamental techniques of the martial art which can be easily learned and remembered – and quickly recalled when needed.

When under severe pressure, your brain will only remember gross motor skills and you will be unable to perform fine technical details due to a range of stress factors. JKD teaches techniques that are effective in such scenarios.

You will be shown the upper body, hand, lower body and leg techniques and how to train them. When you are confident, you will be able to recall and use these basic skills when under pressure.

SPARRING AND FIGHTING

A key training element in developing your skills, we will introduce sparring at a non-contact level and evolve into all-out sparring and fighting against a resisting opponent.

Having a knowledge and experience of hitting someone, evasion, blocking and being hit can give a person advantages in a fight. Experience of sparring and the pressure situations it can bring can help you overcome the initial shock if you ever find yourself in an attack situation.

STREET SMARTS

Prevention is always better than cure, so stopping an attack before it happens is always recommended. You will be taught anti-mugging tactics and how to handle verbal and physical aggression. The benefits of knowing about self-defence and protection strategy can literally save your life.

You will be introduced to the primary natural weapons that we all have – our head, hands, elbows, knees and feet. This section with describe and demonstrate the JKD approach to using them in real situations. These skills can be learned in hours, not days or weeks. They do not require intensive maintenance, although practice is recommended.

While this section looks at the dirty aspects of street scraps, it also considers the aftermath and consequences of such incidents and dealing with the police.

BEING A HAPPY WARRIOR

Using the JKD training to get your mind and body into better shape brings about a sense of achievement and empowerment.

Knowing how to physically hurt someone in a fight and being prepared to defend yourself and your loved ones builds confidence, ability and self-control.

However the training will make you more secure in yourself and less likely to find yourself in situations where violence may occur. In fact, your JKD martial arts training will mean you no longer feel the need – if you did already – to engage in violent confrontations to prove yourself.

Training in JKD can knock the chip off our shoulders. The end result is to be a well-rounded successful individual, who deals well with people, stress and anxiety and the pressures of everyday living.

Knowing and understanding the concepts in this section will improve your life. You will feel stronger and more able to meet challenges in your life and achieve new goals. This progress enables you to give more to your family, friends and community. The result of all this hard work is that you become a Happy Warrior; comfortable in your own skin and ready for any challenge.

APPENDIX

Here you will find your full 12-week strength and conditioning schedule and workouts. Many gym-goers will be familiar with good techniques for each exercise, but if you need a little extra help then please visit www.bodybuilding.com where you will find instructional videos and advice.

This progressive training programme is proven to work and is designed across a six-day workout schedule as follows:

○ Monday, Wednesday and Friday are resistance days
○ Tuesday, Thursday and Saturday are active recovery days
○ Sunday is a rest day to allow the body to fully recover

The book sets out guidelines on the JKD approach to self-protection, personal improvement and healthy ways to live. It is vital to start with the emotional and mental wellbeing approach. If this is not addressed you will not stay the course.

It's important to acknowledge why you train and the fact that most of us do it as a useful hobby to improve our health and wellbeing, fitness and lives.

BRUCE LEE AND PEACE BUILDING IN NORTHERN IRELAND

Hatred and resentment are never far from the surface in Northern Ireland, even though the peace process is more than 20 years old.

One of the things that interested me about Bruce Lee was the way he reacted to sectarianism, racism and hatred.

Simply, he would never hate back. We have used his example for the past 30 years to bring people together in Northern Ireland to train JKD together.

This promotes and makes friendships across the divide in my community and I think that Bruce would have supported this work.

We do this under his wonderful banner......

"Under the stars under the heavens there is but one family"

AUDIT YOUR HEALTH

Before you start training, you need to know about your current state of health. Please complete the short health audit below and the more 'yes' answers, the healthier you are.

☐ Yes ☐ No	Are you a non-smoker?
☐ Yes ☐ No	Do you eat mostly fresh food on a daily basis?
☐ Yes ☐ No	Do you have a balanced diet? At least five portions of fruit and vegetables daily?
☐ Yes ☐ No	Do you drink alcohol moderately?
☐ Yes ☐ No	Are you an appropriate weight for your height?
☐ Yes ☐ No	Can you deal well with stress and pressure in work and life?
☐ Yes ☐ No	Can you relax?
☐ Yes ☐ No	Do you regularly socialise with friends and family?
☐ Yes ☐ No	Can you walk a mile or a kilometre or climb several flights of stairs without feeling out of breath?
☐ Yes ☐ No	Do you exercise for 60 mins a day 5 times per week?
☐ Yes ☐ No	Do you sleep well and wake up feeling good?

INTERPRETING YOUR AUDIT SCORE

If you have answered 'no' to any of the questions, begin by taking positive action to address the issue. For instance, you may need to increase your intake of fresh fruit and vegetables, or ensure that you get about eight hours of sleep each night.

Everyone has positive and negative behaviours in their lives. Positive behaviours include keeping healthy, eating well and maintaining good physical fitness. It's good to have a loving environment for ourselves and our nearest and dearest. It's also advisable to read widely and keep educating ourselves.

Reduce any negative behaviours identified that may include binge eating and drinking, using illegal drugs or substance abuse. Building debts, stressing out, keeping bad company, becoming angry and blaming others may also need to be addressed as they lead to a downward spiral.

Gradually build positive things in your life to replace any negativity. Do it bit by bit and think good thoughts about yourself and others.

LET'S GO

Now you know what we will be covering, let's make a start on how Jeet Kune Do can improve your life.

SECTION 1

THE MINDSET
OF JKD

"I know nothing except the fact of my ignorance"
Socrates

THE MINDSET OF JKD

Many see the physical aspects of a martial art and think it begins and ends there. Sometimes, yes, there is a place for violence in terms of self-protection, but it should not necessarily be the first action.

Jeet Kune Do is as cerebral as it is physical. Being fully aware of your surroundings and the situations you find yourself in are just as important. And using your brain to help and develop others is another important factor in the art.

FIGHT, FLIGHT OR FREEZE

The human body has a default position for dealing with danger. It's called "fight, flight, or freeze". Have you ever frozen with fear and been unable to move? Recognising this feeling and how to overcome it is important.

Such stress responses help us deal with emergencies. But please note, if that response is set off regularly and not managed it can cause health problems.

The feeling of having to deal constantly with problems that are out of your control in your personal and work life can have long-term and very serious consequences, such as a heart problems or depression.

People can pile pressure on themselves due to unrealistic expectations put upon them. This may be because they're afraid they lack physical, intellectual or emotional strengths needed to move forward and constantly seek approval from those around them.

Don't hide your emotions because they may turn into a powder keg of anger and resentment. Learn tolerance and forgiveness where possible. Develop listening and assertiveness rather than anger and hostility.

However, if someone attacks you with violence or a weapon, there is little point in reacting with tolerance – otherwise you may end up maimed or worse.

MY "JOHN WAYNE" MOMENT

I grew up watching John Wayne taking on the baddies of the Wild West.

Aged 18, I had just started work in Dublin and had been training in karate for about six months. I went to a gig one Friday evening, all was going great and I met an attractive young woman. Naturally I embellished my CV, telling her that I was an accomplished martial artist, intellectual and man-about-town. The lady agreed to allow me to walk her home as we both lived in the same area of the city.

But as we walked along the street, we saw two men giving a good kicking to a young man who eventually ran off in a panic. His girl-friend was screaming her head off for help.

We walked on after trying to calm the young woman down as she begged us to look out for her friend. I tut-tutted and said what horrible men they were, wishing I could give them a damn good thrashing. Well, I was about to get my chance to be a knight in shining armour.

We eventually caught up with the two muggers. I said to my companion to walk on, as I was going to challenge these guys and sort them out.

She walked ahead quickly (she had suddenly realised that I was a complete bloody idiot) as I said to the guys: "I suppose you two think you're hard men, do you?" They both said yes!

I immediately let out a kiai warrior shout and tried my best karate reverse punch on the biggest one but nothing happened. I did it wrong and it didn't work. The lads then sneered, kiaied back and proceeded to give me a proper kicking. One held me down while encouraging his mate to kick me in the head as hard as possible. Luckily my head is filled mostly with concrete!

I somehow broke free, we scrambled and I ended up on the ground on top position on the big guy (I did not know about Jiu Jitsu mount position at the time). I was just getting the upper hand when the other one ran over and kicked me again.

I remember stopping to pick up my new trendy slip-on platform shoes, then ran in my sock soles as they chased me. It was like the Keystone Cops.

I glanced back and the buggers now had glass bottles in their hands and they were really mad. I was going to get it if they caught me. I ran faster and darted round a corner, dived over a hedge and hid in a garden. They searched for me, but eventually gave up and walked away.

I waved down a car and the driver gave me a lift. I slowly made my way home, feeling sore and sorry for a few days.

I never saw the young lady or the muggers again. Lesson learned: I don't do John Wayne impressions anymore and learned it's not really the best tactic or advice to face up to muggers and ask them if they are hard men? It's a funny story now but it wasn't funny then.

Street violence is everywhere and you'll see it in the news and on social media every day. JKD self-protection training will increase your mental and physical strength, and your abilities, to overcome such violence if it comes your way.

AWARENESS AND AVOIDANCE OF DANGER

By using your common sense and gut instincts you will be able to keep yourself safe most of the time. However, learning about verbal de-escalation and avoidance as well as counter tactics builds your confidence and gives you the tools to protect yourself and your loved ones in dangerous situations.

It must be said that there are no 100% self-defence solutions – they are for the movies. Reality is different and as instructor Marc Mac Young says:

Einstein's Law of Reality E = Sh*t Happens

Sometimes life throws a lot of bad things our way and just when you think that it's over, it sometimes gets worse. Just deal with it one piece at a time and things will usually improve.

USE COMMON SENSE TO KEEP TROUBLE AT BAY

Visualise potential problems in advance and take steps to avoid them. For instance, parking your car in a place that has lots of cars during the day but is deserted at night when you return will leave you vulnerable. Muggers and opportunists are waiting around these places to strike. Be aware of these little things as they could save you a lot of problems.

Taking a shortcut off the main track may lead you right into the path of the bad guys waiting for easy prey. Watch some wildlife documentaries and see how predators operate in the jungle, because muggers do the very same things in an urban environment.

If you go to places that are edgy or dangerous, or hang around with people who go looking for trouble then expect to find it.

At the start of an evening you and your friends may be in great form. But as the evening progresses – and as alcohol or drugs changes people and lowers their inhibitions – they may say and do things that they would not normally do. This is when trouble and fights occur and a petty childish remark or sleight can get someone badly hurt.

Drink and drugs lessen your awareness and assessment skills. The chances of risk-taking increases. Be careful if you're drinking to not walk around the street like a "buck eejit" as you can meet trouble. A good option is to book a taxi in advance to get you home as wandering around the streets looking for one late at night can be dangerous.

MY "CAGE FIGHT"

A guy called at my home one evening years ago, asking me to help as a doorman for his football team's end-of-season celebrations. I was pretty broke at the time and was glad of the small amount of cash offered.

Myself and two friends were to supervise the door as it was a private party, nothing could go wrong.

As the night wore on the footballers started to have stupid, rowdy arguments. It was shaping up for a messy night. Eventually a group of men banged on the door demanding to come in without tickets We said no and someone threw a pint glass at us, which smashed against the wall. They shouted that they'd be back later.

We thought that was just another empty threat, but the owner came to us later saying that they were at the back door wanting to kick our ass.

The owner was clearly delighted to act as master of ceremonies. He started things off in a metal-barred safety cage he had previously erected at the entrance of the disco. He then stood back to enjoy the fun saying, "Away you go lads".

All hell broke loose and two of us fought the men. At the start, my friend hit one of them with a beautiful right cross and he went down like he had been shot – but he got straight back up again. He started fighting me. I thought, 'Oh f**k, this guy is tough'.

I hit them with punches, knees and elbows, and eventually they just had enough and quit. They had been drinking and were very angry and thought it was a good idea to take us on. It wasn't. I was very fit at the time, loved fighting and even remember stupidly asking the gathered audience: "Who's next?"

There was no response.

I later noticed that my favourite Levi's shirt was ripped off my back. And when I went back into the bar, my other bouncer friend was oblivious to the mayhem and was deep in conversation with a very attractive lady. He was totally embarrassed and we laughed about it later.

MANNERS IN A CLUB OR BAR

Let's say on a night out you bump into someone, spilling their drink. It's best to immediately apologise and move on swiftly. Don't get into an argument. Perhaps offer to buy the guy a replacement drink and be nice.

If you're worried about the situation or possible trouble, speak to a doorman. You may wish to leave immediately and go somewhere else. Don't hang around and don't be a hero or look for trouble because of your ego or loss of face in front of your friend or partner.

If someone stares at you hard and says aggressively, "What the f**k are you looking at?", then apologise, speak to a doorman and consider getting out of there as soon as possible. Don't engage in an argument or a fight if at all possible.

CONTROL THE EGO

I got bumped hard by one of a group of young men while walking down the street in a rough part of London with my girlfriend.

I could have stopped and confronted them. But I didn't. I took it and walked on because if I had stopped, things would probably have turned out nasty for me. I had to let it go in an instant despite my ego was telling me, 'What the f**k! Are you not going to do something?'.

I walked on a bit embarrassed, but so what? Who cares?

BEING BULLIED BY MEN WITH GUNS

When I was a teenager, my friends and I used to get abused and humiliated by British soldiers in Northern Ireland. They would stop us in the street and force us to spread eagle, threaten and assault us on a regular basis.

It was a nightmare living in Northern Ireland at that time. Some of my friends and neighbours were murdered. I hated the humiliation but there was little we could do without it coming back on us.

However it made us and our community very determined to put a stop to it and now the nightmare is over.

MENTAL PREPARATION AND A PROMISE TO YOURSELF

Ask yourself this vital question: 'Am I really prepared to fight all out and do all the necessary things to survive a street assault?'

Take a look on YouTube and see the nasty things that humans do to each other on the street, on a train or bus, and in restaurants, cafés and stores.

The most important promise to make to yourself is that when you walk out your door, you'll be able to walk back in again relatively unscathed. You need to be prepared mentally and physically to defend yourself and your loved ones and to trounce any attacker.

You'll need to train physically to simulate the conditions of a fight scenario because the real world conditions will exhaust you very quickly.

HELPING OTHERS

People often find themselves in a downward spiral, which leads to a string of bad decisions and unfulfilled opportunities. Just having someone there to share their fears and anxieties can make all the difference.

JKD can build the self-confidence and strength needed to take on and combat these obstacles in life – and then teach you to use those very same traits to help others in the same boat.

MY FIRST SOCIAL WORK VISIT

As a new student social worker in London, I was told to go and see a female and her child who were "at-risk" and in some serious trouble. I had not been living in the city long and it was an overwhelming place for me.

I remember feeling anxious at first as I went up in a tower block lift and thought: "What am I going to say to this person? How will I help them?"

When I got to the door, I knocked and the letterbox opened. There was a little girl looking out at me. Then she shouted: "Mummy, there's a white man at the door."

A feeling of panic swept over me initially, but I took a deep breath and paused for reflection before going in. I am glad to say that I was able to help the family with some very traumatic events that had happened in their life. It was one of those moments that helped me to develop and is just unforgettable.

FINDING AND BEING A ROLE MODEL

Many instructors are role models and can walk the talk. They turn up and teach even when they are not feeling well and do the work that no one else wants to do. They organise seminars, clean the mats, empty the trash, register the students and pay the bills.

They take the abuse from parents, irate that their Jim or Julie has not received their belt promotion in time. They are the ones who organise workshops and seminars and take the financial burden when, more often than not, the seminar loses money. However, in reality, a few others are just out to make money and run their organisation like a McDojo or pyramid scheme.

Some have huge egos and seem to be proud of making students suffer. Good coaches lift people up not put them down.

When finding a group or club to join, speak to the instructor and ask about their background. Do your own research on the web afterwards. Think about if you and the instructor have similar attitudes. Speak to the students too, to see what they're attitudes are like. But always be respectful.

PUTTING ON A SEMINAR

I have lost thousands of pounds of my own money on seminar adventures but I don't regret it. One of the first times that I brought in an instructor from the USA, only six people turned up to the event.

I had to pay a large fee plus flights and accommodation and keep my promise to him out of my own pocket.

Some of the top martial arts guys made promises but did not turn up to support me. This has happened on more than one occasion.

It makes me chuckle when I hear people suggest that martial arts instructors should not charge for lessons or take a vow of poverty. Why should we be singled out? Try that tactic the next time you go to the dentist and see what happens.

TAKE INSPIRATION FROM OTHERS

JKD has some high-level role models who have dedicated their lives to improving themselves and educating others in the martial ways; demonstrating better ways to live a positive life, by making a contribution to their communities and society.

These include the founder Bruce Lee, Guro Dan Inosanto, Sigung Taky and Andy Kimura, my dear friend and brother Sifu Alain De Preter and many others.

Such role models while help guide you to help you get out of any downward spiral you find yourself in. They will show you that helping others in the key to success and happiness. And they will intervene when necessary to help bring about a positive change in a person in a respectful way.

COLM'S STORY: HOW JKD HELPED ME COPE WITH A SPINAL INJURY

My passion used to be venture sports and martial arts. I had practiced Kempo Karate since 1975 until my accident five years later. It was a serious accident that resulted in me breaking my back and sustaining a spinal cord injury.

As a wheelchair user, I assumed martial arts was no longer an option for me. Instead, I got involved in scuba diving and kayaking. However, an article in a martial arts magazine reintroduced me to Bruce Lee – and the possibility that Jeet Kune Do might be a real option in self-defence for people with a disability. "Use what works".

I was working as CEO for Spinal Injuries Ireland, based in a large hospital near Dublin. I was developing a venture sports program for individuals who had sustained a spinal cord injury and I thought that if I could learn Jeet Kune Do, I could then introduce it to others with a spinal cord injury.

I contacted a number of different martial artists and trained with a few. There were some who flat-out said those in a wheelchair can't learn martial arts and while most of the others were well-meaning, they too just couldn't see beyond my wheelchair and disability.

They wouldn't listen when I tried to explain the challenges and dynamics of using a wheelchair and how it negated the techniques they were showing.

But my life was changed after reading an article in an American magazine about an instructor who was using JKD to bring the two communities in Northern Ireland together. His name was Martin O'Neill.

People use the term "changed my life" very freely without understanding what it really means. It has changed my life.

I wrote to Martin, hazarding a guess at his postal address, and explained what I was hoping to learn. He responded and said he would love to help in developing a system that worked for wheelchair users and would travel down from Northern Ireland. He saw beyond the wheelchair and disability.

Over the next 16 years Martin travelled down or I went up to him, learning and refining JKD so that it would really work for wheelchair users. It is fair to say that this was a real learning process for both of us.

After a lot of trial and error, we discarded at least 90% of the usual techniques and Martin helped to develop JKD so that it offered real and practical self-defence options for wheelchair users.

Since then, dozens of patients have learned that JKD is not just about martial arts; they gained confidence and have realised that they can be part of the martial arts and wider community.

Learning JKD with Martin was more than just about learning self-defence; it gave me confidence and an insight into challenging the stereotype when people said: "Wheelchair users can't do that."

Over the next 15 years as CEO of Spinal Injuries Ireland, I used the principles I learned with Martin to develop and challenge what the experts said was the norm for wheelchair users.

Thanks to the support of Martin we have developed Wheelchair JKD, an effective self-defence program that has featured in magazines in Ireland, Britain and Europe and I am now an associate instructor. It is a privilege to train with Martin and I count him as a real friend.

Colm Whooley

Associate Instructor

HOW TO INSPIRE OTHERS

Nowadays there is much talk of empowerment, which in reality has to come from within a person. No one can empower you except you. There is no magic wand or pill, and you need to find a way to do this for yourself.

However, if you are an instructor or coach you need to know how to help your students find their inner strength and tap into their hidden resources. Helping the student to help themselves and gradually challenge them to succeed is important and even small changes can lead to bigger success. Remember that few are cut out to be a fighter or Navy Seal; many seek help because they have been bullied or lack confidence.

Making some very small, positive changes to your lifestyle can have a massive impact. For example:

○ take a walk or jog for 10 to 20 mins
○ cut back or cut out the junk food and when in the supermarket don't buy it. If it's not in your cupboard or fridge, it is out of harm's way
○ while waiting for the kettle to boil do 10 squats,10 sit ups and 10 push ups
○ have a light dumbbell to hand and use it while watching TV

Just keep things light at the beginning, but use a diary to keep a note of what you do. Take a look at the end of each week you will be amazed at the progress that you can make in a short time.

A STORY FROM JAMES

Martial arts helped change me from being angry in my youth and into the man I am today. It taught me patience, discipline and improved my physical and mental health. Most of all, it gave me a place to belong. As such, I had already trained in several martial art styles to various degrees of competence by the time I met Martin O'Neill in 2009.

Through a sequence of events that were more than coincidence I found myself at a train station in Northern Ireland shaking his hand. He blew my mind and three hours later, on the train ride home to Dublin, my notebook was filling up. He gave me an inner smile that is still there to this day.

As one of my former instructors put it, I had "found my groove". Martin had put my passion for martial arts back on track and I continued to train with his help. He has also trusted me to pass this on and step outside the boundaries of his teaching, to train with other instructors.

Training in martial arts, and in particular with Martin, has actively and directly helped me deal with the some of the biggest stressors of my life.

In 2012 my wife and son were involved in a major car accident. Luckily, there were no major or lasting physical impacts. But the trauma of the day greatly impacted my wife, who developed post-traumatic stress disorder. This manifests itself in many ways, often through aggressive and even violent outbursts. It has left us both confused, stressed and the ongoing legal process and interviews did not help.

But my training in martial arts has helped me through. Being prepared for violent situations. The discipline, focus and patience I have learned. The support, friendship and camaraderie that comes with being a member of a group such as Martin's JKD Ireland. All of this has in no uncertain terms been responsible for me preserving my own mental health and for helping me to be strong enough to support someone else at their toughest time.

Martin takes a call from me on an almost weekly basis for 30 minutes up to an hour. We mainly talk about martial arts, but it helps so much and brightens that smile inside. He doesn't have to do this, yet he does often and without question.

He has also given me his trust to represent him here in Dublin; to start my own small group and pass on the same skills, insights and values to those who attend my classes. It gives me strength, focuses my mind and pushes me to do my best for them and Martin. It also gives me the ability and strength to be a better husband, father and employee.

In a way, Martin is my lighthouse, shining his light into the storm and offering hope, guidance and friendship. A role model.

HOW TO HELP OTHERS

Giving others a hand up and not a hand out is a great way to give thanks for the changes that you are making in your life. It's fantastic to see others making positive changes to their lives and that you are a part of this change

If someone needs help, give it to them. But don't do it expecting much in the way of thanks. Just give from the heart and don't be judgemental. People who are experiencing difficulties are too busy trying to survive to give you thanks.

For example, it's best to assist the community and voluntary organisations who work with homeless people rather than give directly on the street. Groups like Centrepoint in Soho, London, are really great at helping young homeless people get back on their feet, get accommodation and a job.

HELPING A BOISTEROUS BUNCH OF YOUTHS

I reached out to a group of at-risk teenagers in Northern Ireland and taught them mixed martial arts for 10 weeks.

At the beginning, their concentration levels were zero, which can be frustrating. But as they started to enjoy the programme, they began to connect more and more. They responded well and gained a sense of achievement from it.

The philosophy of JKD is heavily influenced by Bruce Lee, who said: "Under the stars under the heavens we are one family."

Giving something back comes naturally and seeing the bigger picture is possible. The real JKD approach is not about hurting people but helping them to improve themselves and have a better life.

By reaching out and helping others you will find great rewards and a sense of fulfilment in your life. When people are ready for help and support, they may ask for it in a number of ways. Be aware of this and respond positively.

HOW TO COMMUNICATE WELL

Communicating is not all about speaking. Listening to others is an important skill and one that you can develop by giving the speaking person your full attention and displaying good body language.

When having a conversation, do not interrupt the person talking by jumping in mid-sentence. Let them finish before responding.

On meeting someone, they will assess you in about three seconds and spend the next 30 seconds making up their mind about you. Making a good impression from the get-go is therefore important. Don't miss the opportunity.

Experts say that speaking is only about six per cent of communication, with the rest being made up of body language. Develop your skills of communication for success in relationships. Smile (not a goofy fake smile but a natural one) and see how people respond. You'll be surprised as they will generally smile back. Introduce yourself make good eye contact. Smile and say my name is "X" – and try to remember other people's names too.

Keep a good open posture; stand straight and demonstrate confidence and self-awareness even if you're not very confident (fake it till you make it). Take action on these points and don't wait. All these self-presentation points are important when meeting others.

Wondering how to start helping?

Develop your listening skills, especially when listening to your inner voice, your goals and ambitions.

VOLUNTEERING WITH YOUNG MEN AT RISK

While in London, I volunteered with a community youth project one summer on the Broadwater Farm Estate in Tottenham.

This was in a very deprived area and I was one of the few non-black volunteers. I experienced again what it is like to be in a minority.

This was a learning curve for me but, through the empathy and communication skills I have, I did not at any time feel anxious or fearful. I was able to communicate with the young people and got to like them. I think they liked me too.

REACH OUT

Reaching out to people in need should to be done sensitively and carefully, otherwise people may question your motives.

It goes the other way too. If you are having problems, don't allow them to weight you down and worsen. Don't accept that you are a passive victim and alone. Ask for help from family and friends and don't hide your feelings.

Suicide has become increasingly prevalent in recent years, especially in young men who feel under pressure to fit in today's society.

Outwardly, they feel they must show they are successful, fashionable, tough and fit. But underneath, they are perhaps lonely, vulnerable or insecure.

Helping others can also assist with defeating depression or suffering in yourself. If you don't feel able to share a problem or issue with the people close to you, then contact a professional or group. Don't just tolerate the problem.

BULLYING AND JKD: A STORY FROM A BEGINNER

I struggled greatly with having faith in myself. Having been bullied for pretty much as long as I can remember, I had little confidence or belief in myself.

Even when I went to Martin's class for the first time, I thought: "Oh God. I'll never be able to keep up."

I have never been more wrong. I was welcomed into a very friendly group and Martin made sure that I felt comfortable. My life has improved with each lesson and I have taken back my confidence. I've been given the skills that I can apply to almost every aspect of what I do in some way to improve.

It is good to have a teacher who doesn't criticise you at every available opportunity. There is a sense of progress with each lesson and I wish more teachers were like this at all times. I look up to Martin. To say he is humble is an understatement. He speaks highly of his mentors and friends, but always says, "I still have a lot to learn."

I've taken this saying to heart because no matter how good I get at something, I'll still have something more to learn.

Every time I go to a class, I'm guaranteed a story of some sorts from Martin and I love this aspect of being taught something and having a story related to it. Whether it be a funny story about working as a bouncer or training with his Instructors, there is never a dull lesson.

I have been introduced to a wide variety of people who I never would have otherwise met. I couldn't be any more thankful.

HOW TO CONDUCT AN INTERVENTION

Using basic active listening and being present for others is important. While no one should become an overnight expert, counsellor or advisor, getting beyond the presenting problem or issue can really help. Often just listening and not judging a person is all that's needed.

Before an intervention it's important to listen carefully and assess the background, needs and problems to be addressed. Don't be tempted to come up with instant solutions or advice, Be wary of forcing your agenda on a person or group. By listening and facilitating a respectful dialogue, people will usually find their own solutions. Your role is merely to guide or signpost along the way.

Timing is also important as sometimes people are not ready to help themselves or to be helped and will reject you. Don't impose your help or patronise people or you will be seen as a fake or a busybody. People hate this attitude.

In JKD we start with physical training, which gradually becomes more challenging. During training we always have a laugh and after the session we have a chat where anyone can ask questions or be available for one-to-one discussion and support.

My JKD training brings together the physical and more defensive oriented side, together with the emotional and mental strength sides.

 Some instructors just seem to focus on the violence and self-defence. But this is missing some very important issues such as learning about conflict management, self-improvement, empowerment and wellbeing; how to help to improve your life and perhaps someone else's. Reaching out to marginalised young men and women. Coping with depression, bereavement, loss and illness.

WORKING WITH YOUNG "AT-RISK" LADS

I trained a group of teenage boys, who in the beginning had a very short attention span. My job was to keep the sessions lively and not to allow any bullying or top dog or underdog stuff.

We kept changing things and got them to grapple on the ground a lot. They loved this as they probably all watched UFC and knew a few moves. Mostly the illegal ones.

To help prevent bullying, we kept the top dogs on the mat in a "winner-stays-on" format. Eventually, even they got exhausted and gave up. Even the tough guys cannot sustain it forever.

The lads are still attending the Youth Club and seem to be doing OK.

Some are still on the edge but the Youth Leader is helping keep them on track. I am pleased they are mostly alright, yet aware they still have a long way to go.

A JKD approach can give a more holistic support system for individuals to have a better lifestyle, as well as the dynamic physical martial ways.

SECTION 2

JKD TRAINING AND EQUIPMENT

"When your temper rises lower your fists.
When your fists rise lower your temper"
Chojun Miyagi founder of Goju Ryu Karate

JKD TRAINING AND EQUIPMENT

By using your imagination and basic equipment, your training activities can be made into exciting and enjoyable workouts.

Having good-quality, basic training equipment at your disposal is a great way to bring a professional approach to your training.

What we'll look at

- what to buy
- heavy bag training methods
- focus pads techniques
- top and bottom ball
- skipping

PUTTING TOGETHER A STARTER KIT

Having these items in your kit bag or at home will mean you can do a short activity session easily when you have a few spare moments.

Buy the best equipment that you can afford as I've found cheap equipment will let you down in the end. If you're on a tight budget, you can get off to a great start with the following:

- a good pair of focus mitts
- 16oz gloves
- a skipping rope
- a mouth guard
- a heavy bag, if you have the cash

TRAINING CLOTHING

Your training kit for when going to a class should include:

- a clean cotton T-shirt or rash guard
- shorts or long pants

- a good pair of cross trainers (cheap ones will increase risk of injury)
- bring water, a towel and use deodorant – don't be a stinker
- keep nails cut short, don't be a wolfman
- if doing a lot of grappling wear either a clean rash guard, or Jiu Jitsu uniform.
- beware of leaving your training gear in your bag as it will grow bacteria, cause infections and will smell of cat's pee.

BOXING GLOVES

Obtain a good pair of 16 ounce leather boxing gloves. Avoid cheap and nasty plastic gloves as they offer little protection to your hands. Use antiseptic spray to prevent them growing bacteria and stinking with sweat.

FOCUS PADS

Focus pads are a wonderful tool and you will use them at nearly every session. A partner is required for this activity and learning how to feed the pads (holding the pads for your partner to hit) is useful and enjoyable. This builds skill, timing, reflexes and great technique. Start with the front hand, jab from the fighting stance to get the idea.

Some fundamental progressive drills with your focus mitts and heavy bag include the following.

- single jab
- double jab
- triple jab
- jab – cross
- hook
- hook – cross
- jab – cross – uppercut
- jab – cross – two uppercuts
- jab – cross – hook – cross – hook – cross

When practicing, imagine that you're hitting just two inches behind the target area. Allow the body to move naturally and get a good feeling for technique.

In the beginning move slowly, with purpose and gradually build the movement up progressively and smoothly.

Tip: Slow and smooth technique will get faster as your training progresses. Develop fantastic body feel and motion, don't be a robot and remain static. Move smoothly and gracefully, and develop good footwork. Combine this with the pads combinations described above.

Start in two-minute rounds by moving forward, back, left and right, and circle in both directions. As you progress, increase to three-minute rounds as this is more challenging. Always remember to breathe out on the hits and don't flick or push the punches.

HEAVY BAG

The heavy bag is a first class and an underused resource in gyms and homes. At home avoid placing it badly in your garage as it could bring the roof crashing down.

When training a heavy bag session, it's best to wear hand wraps and good bag gloves or 16oz gloves. I don't advise hitting a heavy bag with bare knuckles as it can cause damage to your hands and arthritis can occur in later life.

Visualise the idea of actual combat to get the best from the session. Hit and move. And when the bag comes towards you, hit it and control it with strikes and forearms, elbows and shoulders. Ensure that the wrist is straight on impact or risk injury.

There are different bags available. Some lighter and some heavier, shorter or longer. A standing heavy bag with the base filled with water may be useful as it can be placed outdoors or indoors.

The bags give the opportunity to build your technique.

- ○ single jab
- ○ jab – cross
- ○ jab – cross – hook
- ○ jab – cross – jab

Change your stance from left to right and do it again and time two to three minutes for several rounds.

TOP AND BOTTOM BAG

A top and bottom bag has elastic bands on each end and is connected to the ceiling and floor with a clip or kettlebell. When hit, it moves around erratically and is great for timing hand shots, back fist, chops, and even light kicks. When it's not fitted too tightly, it moves in more unpredictable ways and when hit hard can bounce back swiftly to smack your face, which can be funny.

BOB DUMMY

A BOB dummy resembles the top half of a man and is made of hard rubber. It's a useful and fun device for practicing hitting and various strikes to targets such as the face and neck and ribs. BOB never complains.

RESISTANCE BANDS AND SKIPPING

Resistance bands are very handy and portable as they don't need much space. You can pack them into your suitcase and workout when on holiday.

A skipping rope is also inexpensive and portable. Skip in rounds of two and three minutes and develop light and fast footwork, coordination and endurance.

Build a nice tempo and gradually increase the pace. Take a look at YouTube videos of old school boxers such as Muhammad Ali for inspiration.

USING A MIRROR

Shadow sparring into a mirror is a helpful way to see your "magnificent technique". Practice in slow motion at the start and do the hand and kicking combinations, viewing your technique. Then go at half and finally full speed.

YOGA

Basic yoga is recommended as it keeps the body mobile and agile as the years advance and a yoga mat is portable.

TRAINING ON DIFFERENCE SURFACES

- ○ working on a bare floor is good, as is a matted floor, depending on the aims of the training session.
- ○ using rough terrain and the street is sometimes advisable as you don't know where an attack may happen.
- ○ it's best to be prepared for a wide variety of situations.

A NOTE ON MARTIAL ARTS ACADEMIES

There are many martial arts to choose from and many clubs or instructors within. Search for one that's practical, accessible, and able and gives good value for money. Speak to the instructor, ask questions about their background and find out whether he/she is legitimate. Check it on the web later.

See for yourself if you like the instructor and their attitude. Speak to the students to see if they're friendly and approachable. If they're arrogant or cocky, that's generally a bad sign. Always be very respectful when attending or visiting a school because you are being assessed as well.

BEWARE OF FRAUDS AND NUT CASES

The martial arts have a fair share these people, many of whom appear to live in a fantasy land. Beware of "psycho instructors" who are egotistical and out to hurt people, or constantly talk about how tough they are. My advice is don't train with them as they may use you for target practice.

There are lots of regular martial arts available now, but few JKD Instructors or classes. Many martial arts are sports-oriented and competition-based, and depend upon lots of children to have an income. JKD is more martial arts and self-defence based and we have a small number of students.

While I admire certain aspects of mixed martial arts (MMA), I don't really appreciate some of the sport's approach. The work ethic of the athletes is very impressive. However, I find it sometimes tends to lack respect, fuels big egos and trash talking. I have noticed children being influenced the wrong way with the disrespectful attitudes and macho swearing, which I find unacceptable.

I enjoy the JKD martial arts that we do as it's pretty real. It has a practical application, a combative mentality and as the years fly past, the old school JKD suits me.

Its tactics and systems can be modified to support older people who aren't so dynamic or physical as their younger counterparts.

In the end, it's really your choice to decide what you want to do. Choose what suits your personality, age, abilities, needs and interests, and the route you want to take.

SECTION 3

INTRODUCTION TO THE WORKOUTS

"When in doubt train"
Erik Paulson

INTRODUCTION TO THE WORKOUTS

As mentioned earlier in the book, you will be taken through a practical and challenging, progressive series of activities and training over a 12-week period.

The detailed breakdown of day-to-day and week-to-week activities can be found in the appendices, but here is an outline of the three components of the programme.

The idea is to give you the best start to your training and take you up to the next level of fitness and conditioning.

HOW THE 12 WEEKS ARE STRUCTURED

PHASE 1: WEEKS 1-3

This is where you set the scene for the new you to begin.

You should complete a basic medical assessment before you start. If required, ask someone to help such as a doctor or health/fitness professional.

This first evaluation on day one is used to assess any physical problems, health or medical issues. It's used to measure your weight, height, waist, chest, arms, legs, and body-fat ratio. It also helps you to evaluate your starting points, assess flexibility and any injuries or problems.

Make a note of these statistics. At the end of each week you can reassess this record and make a note in your diary. Doing this is important to track and evaluate your progress.

During weeks 1-3, the basic workouts are tailored to suit your one repetition maximum (the heaviest weight you can lift) for the weight training schedule. You may feel a bit sore and stiff the day after the exercises, like you do when you tackle a big digging job in the garden.

This is normal as your body becomes accustomed to the activities, and should pass within a day or two.

PHASE 2: WEEKS 4-7

In this phase, the activities and exercises are gradually increased to be more challenging and more variety is introduced.

PHASE 3: WEEKS 8-12

In this phase, the activities and exercises become even more varied and demanding as you become fitter and stronger. Now your body is responding even better to the challenges before you and is becoming able to meet these head on, so the exercises need to become more taxing to reflect that.

GYM WORKOUT ADVICE

BARBELLS AND DUMBBELLS

A few pieces of equipment are required to get started. Versatile types of equipment include a light barbell and dumbbells to do simple and compound exercises. A simple exercise is a dumbbell curl and a compound exercise involves many more body parts working together, such as a squat.

These bits of kit are widely available, pretty cheap and handy to have around.

RESISTANCE MACHINES

Some hardcore people refuse to use machines, but I recommend both free weights and machine workouts. Machines are easy to use even if movement is somewhat restricted. However, they are safe to use and user friendly when you get acquainted with them.

Initially, I wouldn't use machines but now I don't do very heavy lifting workouts, they are a handy way of mixing up exercising, which saves time. However machines are expensive and large and most people can't afford to have them in their homes, so you'll have to travel to a gym to use them.

ADAPTATION FOR HOME

Home training can be done with some basic equipment. However, please be careful not to waste money as I have seen many home gyms later become clothes horses.

SIMPLE HOME WORKOUT SUGGESTIONS

You can get a great basic workout with just bodyweight exercises.

Sets: 3 to 5 Repetitions: 10

WORKOUT 1

Progression: AMRAP (as many repetitions as possible)

- Squats (Tip: add a light dumbbell in each hand for progression)
- Abdominal crunches
- Press ups
- Thrusters
- Chair tricep dips

HOME WORKOUT 2

- 3 min warm up slow shadow sparring
- 1x2 min shadow sparring punches
- 1x2 min kicking
- 1x2 min knees and elbows
- repeat above as required
- stretch for 3 minutes

HOW TO EXERCISE SUCCESSFULLY

- ○ decide on a training schedule and plan times that suit you
- ○ build this into your everyday life, even for a few minutes each day
- ○ take small progressive steps towards your goals every session
- ○ build this up every week and month
- ○ find a training partner to help with motivation and enjoyment
- ○ if you miss a session don't worry just get back on track the next time
- ○ reward yourself on your rest day, but not with lots of junk food or drink
- ○ if you binge or mess up, just get back on track the next day

CALCULATE YOUR ONE REPETITION MAXIMUM (1RM)

Your 1RM is the maximum amount of weight you can lift for any given exercise. It's important to know for the exercises such as deadlift, squat and bench press. If this is a problem, speak with your trainer.

You will be asked to lift weights at a certain percentage of your 1RM and then track your progression. You will see in the workouts in the appendices that there are exercises at 80% or 60% of 1RM, so do the maths in advance.

METHOD

Take each weight 1RM and use 60% of this to have as a benchmark for all sets to be lifted in Phase 1.

When you start Phase 2, add 2.5 kilograms (approx. 5lbs) to the bar. Do the same at the start of Phase 3.

Don't be tempted to add more weight too soon or you run the risk of injury and developing poor form in technique, which is a very bad habit. Don't go above 80% of your maximum to be on the safe side during this programme.

CALCULATE YOUR MAXIMUM HEART RATE (MHR)

The quick and easy way to calculate your maximum heart rate is with this simple, but approximate, formula:

○ MHR = 220 minus your age. The typical training zone is between 60 to 70% of your maximum heart rate

○ However, if you have a heart or health condition this may be drastically lowered to perhaps 30 or 40% and you will still gain health and fitness benefits from a regular training programme

○ Please consult your Doctor or health professional about this issue if it's a worry.

ASSESS YOUR RATE OF PERCEIVED EXERTION (RPE)

If you don't have a heart rate monitor to hand, another technique is to use a psycho-physiological method called the "rate of perceived exertion".

Perceived exertion is how hard you feel your body is working. It's important to note that the rating you give any particular level of effort is based on all the physical sensations you experience during activity, such as:

○ increased heart rate
○ increased respiration or breathing rate
○ increased sweating
○ the burning sensation you get with muscle fatigue.

It is sometimes called the Borg Scale after its creator, Dr Gunnar Borg, who said: "Although this is a subjective measure, a person's exertion rating may provide a fairly good estimate of the actual heart rate during physical activity."

Through experience of monitoring how your body feels, it will become easier to know when to adjust your intensity, especially when you cross-reference with a heart rate monitor. It takes a little practice but it's a great skill to master.

HOW TO USE THE RPE SCALE

When doing physical activity, feel and rate your perception of exertion. Remember, this should reflect how demanding the exercise feels to you combining all sensations and feelings of physical stress, effort and fatigue.

Don't concern yourself with any one factor, such as burning legs or shortness of breath, but try to focus on your total feeling of exertion.

Tip: Pick a number. When you're exercising, choose the number that best describes your level of exertion. It's a good idea to memorise this scale or print it and stick it up near the piece of cardiovascular equipment you're using so it's easy to refer to.

RPE	DESCRIPTION AND HEART RATE
Level 0	nothing at all, resting heart rate 60 to 75 bpm
Level 1-2	Very easy
Level 3-4	Moderate, can do for up to 60 mins MHR 60%
Level 5-6	Harder, can do up to 30 mins MHR 70%
Level 7-8	Very hard, can do for a few mins MHR 80%
Level 9	Almost as hard as possible MHR 90%
Level 10	Absolutely flat out 100% can do for a few seconds only

This rating will give you a good idea of the intensity level of your activity and you can use this information to speed up or slow down your movements to reach your desired range.

Try to appraise your feeling of exertion as honestly as possible without thinking about what the actual physical load is. Your own feeling of effort and exertion is important, not how it compares to other people. Look at the scale and the descriptions and then pick a number. Remember to push your limits a little more at every session otherwise you will be standing still or going backwards.

ACTIVATE YOUR BODY WITH PULSE RAISERS

Raising your pulse in a warmup can be achieved in numerous ways, for example:

- jogging
- skipping
- shadow boxing
- body weight exercises

The idea is to get ready for the training session and not to go all out just yet. After four minutes of activity you should feel just slightly puffed with perhaps a light sweat.

TIP: Activate the body with JKD techniques

- 3 minutes slow to medium speed shadow kickboxing
- hands x 30 secs
- elbows x 30 secs
- knees x 30 secs
- low line kicking x 30 secs
- gradually raise the tempo

The beauty of this is that you are working actual techniques and so save time on mastering punches and kicks.

BUILD YOUR CORE STRENGTH

Core stability training is widely used in modern fitness and is considered to be an important part of most training programmes.

Simply put, core stability holds the trunk and centre of the body to steady the movement of the arms and legs.

Problems arise due to people having poor posture or excessive sitting at work or in leisure time. This weakens core muscles, and good training methods help restore them.

These exercises require stabilisation in the legs, trunk and body and are useful in core stability training:

- plank
- rowing on a cable machine
- standing shoulder press
- Swiss ball exercises
- kickboxing
- Brazilian Jiu jitsu and grappling

STRETCHING

The modern, sedentary lifestyle leads the body to lack mobility and muscles lose their suppleness over time. Before and after working out, mobilise the body with a short active stretching session.

This is important to avoid excessive stress and strain when transitioning from an inactive to an active lifestyle.

Stretching before and after a workout helps to prevent delayed onset muscle soreness (DOMS), keeps you supple and flexible. and prevents injuries.

Overstretching will do more harm than good, so stretch gently, gradually and correctly. Think of your muscles as rubber bands. Pull too hard and it may tear.

Don't compete with others when stretching. Everyone is different and you must listen to your body and relax into the stretch. It takes regular daily practice to stretch, so be patient if you want to improve and avoid injury. Remember that a few minutes a day stretching is better than a one-hour stretch once a week.

HOW TO WARMUP AND STRETCH

Why does warming up matter? A good warm up gets the body and mind activated for the workouts ahead as it increases the flow of blood around the body and gets the cardiovascular system more active.

This then increases the flow of synovial fluid to lubricate the joints as the body warms up and this is a great time to stretch.

What sort of things are part of a good warm up and stretch? Warm ups can start from the top of the head down to the toes on a gradual and flowing sequence.

Start gently with the neck looking left and right and up and down for a series of 10 repetitions followed by these exercises, holding stretches for up to 30 seconds as you progress:

ACTIVITY	DESCRIPTION
arm swings	10 reps
shoulder rolls	10 reps
waist turns	10 reps
forward, back and side bends	10 reps
hamstring stretch	10 secs
quadriceps stretch	10 secs
calf stretch	10 secs
full squats	10 reps
bend forward and touch toes	10 secs

TAKE PHOTOS

Every Friday morning at the same time, before breakfast and after you have gone to the toilet, take a look at yourself in the mirror.

Take time to notice your changing shape as you move towards being a more healthy, toned and fitter person.

Take a photo each week as this will help to record your progress. People will notice you differently and give you compliments, which is nice.

SECTION 4

FUNDAMENTAL TECHNIQUES OF JKD

"Train hard fight easy"
Alexander Suvorov

FUNDAMENTAL TECHNIQUES OF JKD

There is no definite, 100% proven way of winning a fight. However in JKD there is a progressive training methodology designed to give you the edge.

The training system will enable you to achieve excellent results, but you have to have patience, faith in yourself, be consistent and train daily.

Results will come in weeks and months, not instantly. Take time to enjoy the process, work hard and smart.

The basic techniques in JKD can be easily learned and remembered. The reason being, that when under severe pressure you'll only remember gross motor skills and won't be able to perform fine technical details. This is due to stress factors, adrenaline flooding your body, tunnel vision and auditory impairment.

In this section you will be shown:

- O the JKD fighting stance
- O footwork drills
- O upper body tools
- O lower body tools
- O how to start putting them together
- O how to train with the correct mindset
- O having the confidence to fight back

JKD has solid basic techniques which are easy to learn and quick to apply. A person doesn't have to be in prime athletic shape at the start, as the training will help towards this.

Have you ever seen an out-of-shape older guy or woman handing a verbal or physical beat down to a younger fitter man? That's about experience, body language and confidence.

Remember that basic JKD is simple, direct, effective and not difficult to master.

WHAT ARE THE BEST JKD STRATEGIES AND TACTICS

This book is focused upon what works and not the latest fashion and fad in martial arts and training methods. Using strategy and tactics will develop quick thinking and response time to problems. These range from the legal and moral aspects of combat, threat awareness and confrontation management.

Only when you have gained inner strength, confidence and competence to use your full abilities can you hope to succeed. Especially in a challenging, threatening situation and generally in life.

In a fierce confrontation, confidence and ability to act is paramount – not the amount of fancy moves that you have learned in the gym.

You won't remember the complex techniques or moves. Fine motor skills will disappear in the mist of an adrenaline rush and tunnel vision. You will only remember the gross motor skills and techniques learned and drilled thousands of times and under lots of pressure.

Note the word "thousands". Drilling a few techniques once a week will be of no use when the chips are down and you and your loved ones are in danger.

In the training, use of environmental awareness and combat tactics with one-to-one and multiple opponents are important to understand. On the street, fighting for your life is very different than in a ring and this will be explained.

'FIRE HOSING' AND THE WESTERN MIND

Deluging – or fire hosing – someone with lots of techniques at once is not the best way to learn. "Show the everything quickly and you show them nothing," one instructor once boasted, thinking he was smarter than everyone else.

Learn the basics by keeping it simple. Learn a few workable and effective techniques and keep them sharp in your body and mind. Keep pressure testing yourself and your skills and you will own them.

Use common sense. Don't get carried away with the latest fad and fashion. Putting 100% effort into training is the only way to get better. Don't use the training session as a mere social gathering, get down to business and you will improve. Use sets of 10 to 100 repetitions and gradually these build into skills done thousands of times, which brings real mastery.

One problem with the Western mind is that as soon as we see a new technique, we think about countering it without first spending time learning it. Bruce Lee evaluated and analysed everything carefully and with scientific rigour and wanted his students to do the same, not just merely 'do' because he had said so.

Have patience and really examine the skills and techniques. Learn and play with them to see how each one works for you. Then consider if you can apply them under real pressure. After careful evaluation you may wish to keep, modify or discard some of them or a lot of them.

For example, a young person may effortlessly do a high kick but as they grow older they may not have the athleticism to pull it off effectively and may have to modify this and kick much lower.

Trying to compete full-on with an athletic 20-year-old in Brazilian Jiu Jitsu is a complete and utter waste of time if you're over 40 unless you're a high grade or BJJ black belt. You need to think and act differently, as you will quickly gas out and get smashed.

TECHNIQUES

The following section describes JKD footwork, on guard and basic upper body techniques performed by the hands, forearms and elbows.

THE JKD 'ON GUARD' POSITION

Learn the on guard position and how to use it to your advantage.

Spend time getting this position correct and develop the ability to move into the on guard swiftly and economically. The on guard position uses the idea of the angle stance and the old school JKD approach uses "power side" or strongest side forward.

Training this way enables a person to do the maximum damage with the lead tools of their body. That said, do aim to keep your body in balance. You will need to train both sides of your body to be prepared for all situations. Don't become a one sided fighter.

The modified on guard position

The stance can be slightly modified into a less aggressive-looking one simply by opening the palms at head height to face outward towards the opponent. It then looks non-threatening but is actually a strong defensive posture.

A key idea is connected to the principle of, "Longest weapon to the nearest target." This is best illustrated by the finger jab to the eye or throat, and the lead leg kick to the knee or groin. These blows are all long range ones. They are very painful and time needs to be spent developing them into potent weapons in your arsenal.

A mobile fighting stance enables you to move quickly and efficiently in all directions. All of the main footwork movements are practiced from this stance. Think of the idea of the points of a compass, moving north, south, east, west, in a smooth, gliding series of movements.

USE FOOTWORK TO BAMBOOZLE AND OUTWIT YOUR ENEMY

Without good footwork, a JKD practitioner is like a tank chasing a rabbit.

Don't just stand there taking punishment and ruining your good looks by getting beaten up. Use your footwork to stay out of trouble and be the one dishing out the punishment to any opponent.

Good footwork enable you to hit without being hit, which is one of the most demoralising things that you can do to an opponent. Don't be a fool by thinking this bit is boring; it could save you from a beating.

Footwork gives you the opportunity to dictate the pace and completely dominate and clobber an opponent. It is frustrating not being able to track down and hit an opponent. This is can make your opponent angry. If this happens and they lose self-control, the battle is easily won.

For more success, place proper emphasis on footwork and mobility training.

HAND TECHNIQUES AND ON GUARD STANCE ADVICE

In JKD the hands are the primary weapons and tend to do about 70% of the work. Some of the most important techniques to master in the beginning are the following:

- jab
- cross
- hook
- lead straight punch
- finger jab
- back fist

STEP-BY-STEP INSTRUCTIONS AND GUIDELINES

Remember, everything starts with proper on guard posture and a well-balanced mobile stance.

- keep relaxed and ready, not tense
- brain focused on the task
- eyes on target
- hands up to protect head

- don't clench your fists
- shoulders up
- chin down
- elbows tucked in
- lead hand in front
- aim striking hand at target
- think of the arm as the barrel of a gun and punches as bullets
- rear hand near the jaw
- body at an angle (don't stand square in front of opponent)
- abdomen flexed
- knees slightly bent
- weight 50/50 on each leg
- front foot turned in slightly
- rear foot pointing forward
- rear heel slightly raised

TIPS ON PUNCHING

- keep hands half open and close just before impact when punching
- to make a fist, close the fingers and place the thumb across them, not in between.
- don't keep fists bunched up, it slows the techniques
- keep wrist and back of hand in a straight line
- punch with horizontal fist, palm down, for basic boxing technique
- aim right at target (nose/jaw)
- punch with a snapping impact blow or a deeper hit through the target
- snap arm back to start position
- always keep hands up high to protect the head (computer centre)
- keep good posture, balance
- don't back away in a straight line
- move at an angle

FOR PRACTICE

○ remember to work on both sides of your body
○ start slow and smooth, learn the motion then speed up gradually
○ if there are multiple techniques drill one, then move onto the next
○ work with a partner is recommended
○ use focus pads
○ use heavy bag
○ start with 100 repetitions
○ then do 500 repetitions
○ build up to 1,000 repetitions
○ build up to 10,000 – this is the way to mastery

Next is a description of each basic technique.

JAB

This is a fast snap, stinging punch used to keep the enemy from getting set to attack. Punch him right on the nose, then punch him again to frustrate him and keep him off balance. Keep jabbing him don't let him rest or regroup, harassment is key.

Jab	
Start	On guard
Target	Nose or jaw
Technique	1. On guard 2. Hands up 3. Chin down 4. Elbows in 5. Aim hand at target 6. Make a fist, palm down or vertical 7. Step forward an instant before you hit 8. Snap the punch, hit target with a stinging blow 9. Snap arm back to start position 10. Keep good posture, balance
Close	11. Return on guard 12. Use focus pads or heavy bag with partner swap sides/change roles

The lead jab is a basic bread and butter punch and needs to be practiced at each training session. Keep hands half open and make a fist just before impact. Line up the target with the lead forearm, wrist, fist in line.

This is great for focus pad or heavy bag practice, you can try out a variety of jab sequences as described.Multiple front hand jabs help you think about extra shots you can throw in quickly and provide variety in your training. Common ones to practice are

○ single jab
○ double jab
○ triple jab

Start slowly to feel the pathway and then speed up. Use a vertical or horizontal fist. Practice both and decide which one you like best.

LEAD STRAIGHT PUNCH

The lead straight punch is one of the back bone techniques of JKD which should be well learned and practiced often.

Lead straight punch	
Start	On guard
Target	Nose or jaw
Technique	1. On guard 2. Hands up 3. Chin down 4. Elbows in 5. Aim at target 6. Use a vertical fist 7. Whip punch through target 8. Pivot on rear foot 9. Explode into the movement 10. Whip arm back in a "short arc" return
Close	11. Return to on guard 12. Use focus pads with a partner swap sides/roles

Unlike the jab, the lead hand punches right through the target and finishes with a short whipping action. Use the nose/jaw as a guiding target.

Pivot the rear foot and twist hip and shoulder into the punch explosively. Make a short arc return into the on guard position, ready to attack again.

This punch will give a practitioner a tremendous force to attack an opponent. The lead straight punch should be practiced constantly to make it a potent weapon in the JKD practitioners arsenal.

LEAD FINGER JAB

The fastest JKD technique, used as a last resort to attack the opponent's eyes or throat. The intention is not to blind, but cause a reaction or flinch. When this happens, you can hit again or escape.

Lead finger jab	
Start	On guard
Target	Eyes or throat
Technique	1. On guard 2. Hands up 3. Chin down 4. Elbows in 5. Aim hand at target 6. Bend fingers slightly 7. Thumb tucked in 8. Flick fingers, hit target very fast 9. Snap arm back
Close	10. Return on guard 11. With partner use a piece of A4 paper or card to practice finger jab, swap sides / roles

The finger jab comes from on guard position with no preparation and moves extremely fast to hit the target. Fingers are slightly tensed and open a little or closed to attack the eyes or closed to attack the throat. When aiming at the throat, hold your fingers bunched together and slightly bent, thumb in. This gives maximum protection and added strength to the technique.

THE NARROW PIPE IDEA

To make your JKD hand techniques more efficient and effective, imagine your arm is travelling through a narrow pipe. This will enable you to be more efficient in delivery of straight line techniques.

Using this concept stimulates the economy of motion in the strike to the target. Don't allow your lead elbow to rise up much to the side as this is a dead giveaway and signals the intention to attack.

REAR CROSS

The rear cross punch is a tried and tested power punch with knockout potential and should be a staple of your arsenal.

Rear cross	
Start	On guard
Target	Chin or jaw
Technique	1. On guard 2. Hands up 3. Chin down 4. Elbows in 5. Aim at target 6. Make a horizontal or 45-degree fist before impact 7. Snap rear fist from on guard position 8. Front hand retracts to guard jawline 9. Punch in straight line through target 10. Stay relaxed 11. Drive forward on rear leg 12. Twist hips, shoulder sharply into punch 13. Snap arm back 14. Return on guard
Close	15. Return on guard 16. Use focus pads, heavy bag, partners swap sides/ change roles

The rear cross starts with the rear hand near the shoulder and jawline with the elbow in. It moves fast in a perfect straight line to the target, usually the jaw or chin of the opponent.

Push hard off the rear foot with the energy moving up through the legs, hip, shoulder and arm, wrist and fist. Torque the hip for full effect as it smashes through, relax and don't tense or muscle the punch. It uses the full reach of the arm at extension, but do not fully lock out the arm.

Keep other hand up near the jaw for protection. Return it fast in a straight line to on guard position and don't let it wave around or drop on the way back.

LEAD STRAIGHT PUNCH TO THE BODY

This technique can drive a hard punch between the opponents guard to the solar plexus and drop him.

Lead straight punch to the body	
Start	On guard
Target	solar plexus or groin
Technique	1. On guard 2. Hands Up 3. Chin down 4. Aim at target 5. Make a horizontal fist 6. Punch downward with front hand to solar plexus/groin 7. Bend knees slightly 8. Keep rear hand high 9. Hit through target 10. Snap arm back
Close	11. Return on guard 12. Use focus pads or heavy bag with partner swap sides/roles

The lead straight to the body uses a quick drop step and punch to the groin or solar plexus with the front hand. To be successful, it requires a fast change of level to surprise the opponent and get inside his guard.

Keep your eyes on the opponent at all times and beware of hitting someone with a big beer belly in the gut – it's pure fat and acts like armour plating.

HOOK PUNCH

Used as a counterpunch to get round your opponent's defence or in a combination hooks are a great weapon to master.

Hook punch	
Start	on guard
Target	Jaw / lower ribs
Technique	1. On guard 2. Hands up 3. Chin down 4. Elbows in 5. Aim hand at target 6. Raise elbow upward with fist, wrist, forearm all in line 7. Make a 90 or 45-degree angle with arm 8. Hook punch through side of jaw 9. Torque body twisting into punch, pivot sharply on front foot 10. Hook punch through side of jaw 11. Avoid swinging 12. Hit to centreline of head, no further 13. Snap arm back
Close	14. Return on guard 15. Use focus pads with partner swap sides / roles

The hook is a devastating counterpunch delivered with no preparation in a "whirring arc" motion to the jaw or body of an opponent. It can be delivered with a horizontal or vertical fist.

It's deceptive and can snake around the opponent's guard. However, don't swipe or swing as this telegraphs the punch and puts you out of position.

Keep the guard up and pivot on your hips inward turning the lead foot inward, as you punch, keeping the elbow tight and shoulder high. Punch to the centre line and not beyond this as it leaves you open for counters.

PALM STRIKES

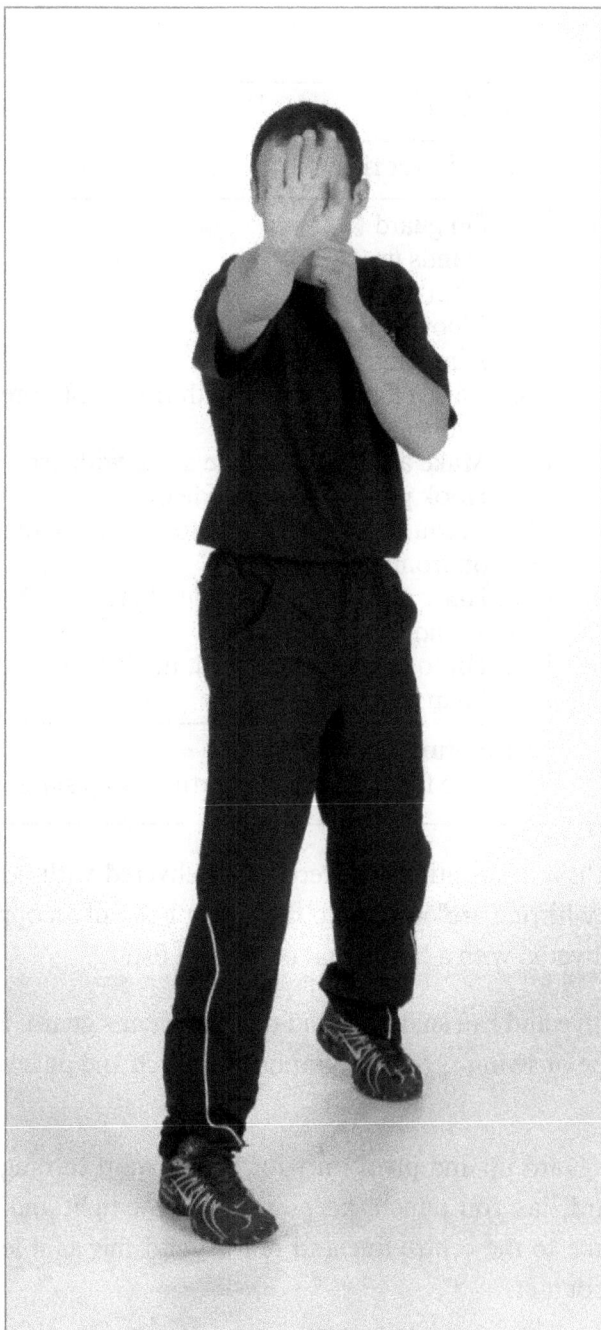

Palm strikes are highly recommended for self-defence as they reduce the risk of damaging your hands compared to closed fist strikes. They are versatile and very easy to learn. Used properly they can end a confrontation super quick.

Palm strike (vertical)	
Start	On guard
Target	Nose or jaw
Technique	1. On guard 2. Hands up 3. Chin down 4. Elbows in 5. Aim hand at target 6. Hand vertical fingers pointing upward 7. Front hand snaps forward 8. Strike forward through target 9. Keep hand open 10. Fingers slightly bent 11. Hit with base of the hand where it joins the wrist 12. Snap arm back
Close	13. Return to on guard 14. Use focus pads with partner swap sides /roles

Delivered as a straight or circling and slapping motion, they can do a lot of damage. Try hitting the focus pads or a well-padded partner with a palm strike and you will be amazed at how hard you can deliver blows in a straight or circling hooking motion.

Cycle the motion and hit several times to gain better results. In combat, if it's working, do it more until you finish the altercation. If it ain't broke don't fix it.

BACK FIST (BASIC)

The back fist is a surprise attack that hits the opponent's jaw hinge, temple or nose with lead hand.

Back fist	
Start	On guard
Target	Jaw hinge/temple
Technique	1. On guard 2. Hands up 3. Chin down 4. Elbows in 5. Aim at target 6. Keep wrist and forearm in straight line 7. Hit with back of knuckles 8. Whip back fist in a short snapping arc with lead hand 9. Strike at a 45-degree angle (not horizontally) 10. Aim through target 11. Snap arm back
Close	12. Return on guard

BIG BACK FIST

The "Big back fist" is a non-whipping, arcing blow that smashes into the opponent. It may be a bit telegraphic but when it hits it'll cause a lot of damage.

Back fist	
Start	On guard
Target	Jaw
Technique	1. On guard 2. Hands up 3. Chin down 4. Elbows in 5. A similar movement to back fist 6. Smash through 8 jawline 7. Explosively torque shoulders, hips pivot feet 8. Hit with knuckles 9. Snap back
Close	10. Return on guard 11. Use focus pads swap with partner change/roles

The back fist is a great weapon if the opponent blocks your straight punch, you can roll it over hitting him and trap his arm with your other hand. Don't hit his hard skull as your will injure your knuckles. The picture shows trapping of the arm and a back fist to the jaw. Note the lead leg jam pushing forward to unbalance him.

HAMMER FIST

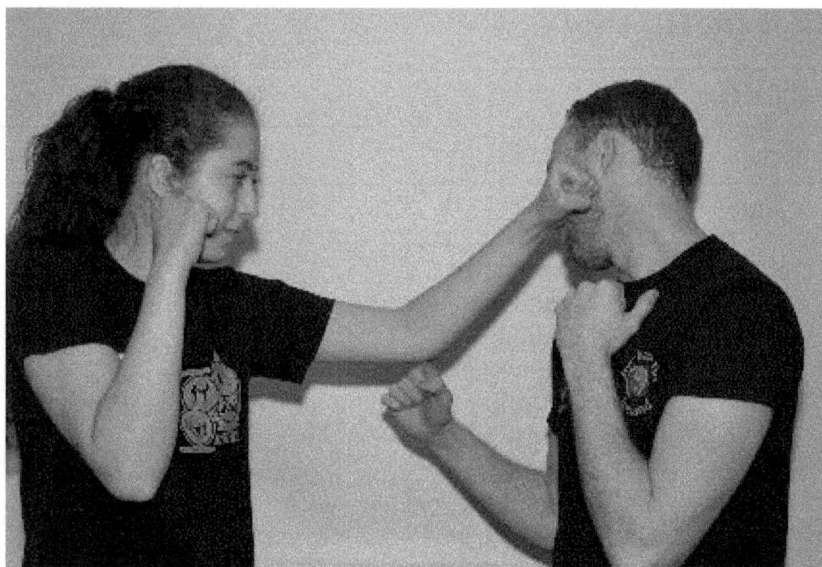

Hammer fist uses the area at the bottom of the fist which minimises the risk of your hand being injured.

Hammer fist	
Start	On guard or arms by side of body
Target	Jaw
Technique	1. On guard 2. Hands up 3. Chin down 4. Elbows in 5. Aim at target 6. Make a fist 7. Hit with bottom of fist 8. Use backhand or forehand strike 9. Hit through target 10. Torque shoulder and hip 11. Snap back
Close	12. Return on guard 13. Use focus pads with partner swap sides/roles

ELBOW STRIKES

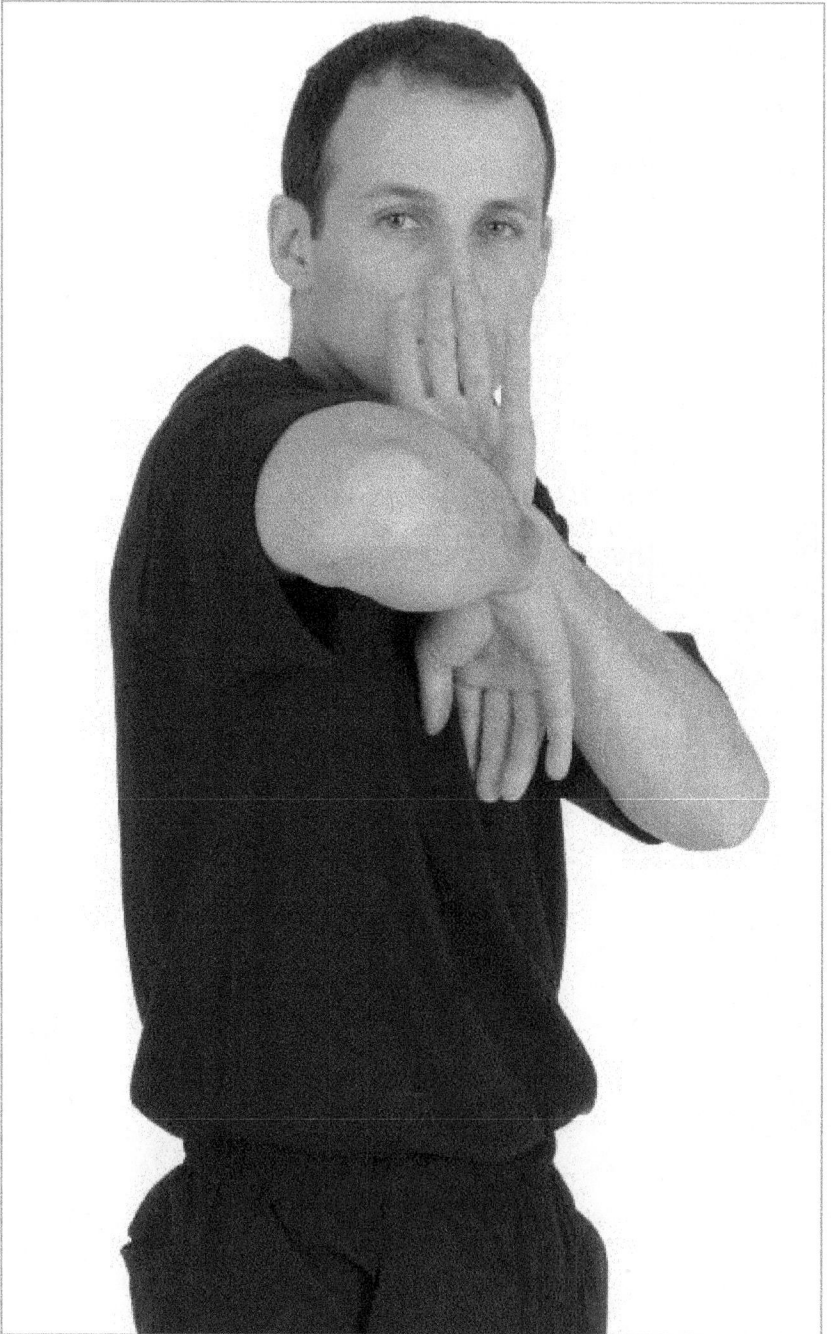

Elbows are a brilliant tool for smashing an attacker at close range. They can be used at any age; even elderly people can use them easily. They are versatile and easy to remember and repeat under duress.

Elbow strikes	
Start	On guard
Target	Jaw
Technique	1. On guard 2. Hands up 3. Chin down 4. Elbows in 5. Aim at target 6. Raise elbow horizontally 7. Hit elbow through jaw line 8. Torque body, hip and shoulder 9. Pivot front foot towards target 10. Snap back
Close	11. Return on guard 12. Use focus pads/ Thai pads with partner swap sides/roles

Elbow strikes are easy to learn and may be delivered in many directions. Horizontal elbow across and diagonal down are important ones. I recommend learning the bread and butter horizontal elbow first and the diagonal down next.

Use the bony part of the elbow to hit, keeping your hand open and relaxed (not clenched and closed).

Elbows are extremely devastating blows delivered at close range to the jaw, temple and body. They are part of a group of techniques including headbutts and knees that are easily learned and don't require a lot of maintenance.

UPPERCUTS

Uppercut range is close quarter, when you are in arm's length of the opponent or have crashed inside his guard. If you are here you must be attacking don't be passive, as it's a danger if you are not properly aware.

Uppercut	
Start	On guard
Target	Jaw
Technique	1. On guard 2. Hands up 3. Chin down 4. Elbows in 5. Aim at target 6. Make a fist 7. Bend knees, dip down 8. Make 90 degree angle with arm 9. Knuckles facing away 10. Strike upward under chin 11. Hit through target 12. Snap back
Close	13. Return on guard 14. Use focus pads horizontally, partner, / swapping roles / swap sides

Imagine forming the letter U as this helps to describe an uppercut. They are delivered with no preparation in an upward motion. It's delivered up from the legs, through the body and arms to the target's chin/jaw.

Don't swing or swipe, or hit too high, it blocks your vision by stopping the punch at your eyeline. Keep arms tight when executing the uppercut for attack and defence.

OVERHAND PUNCH

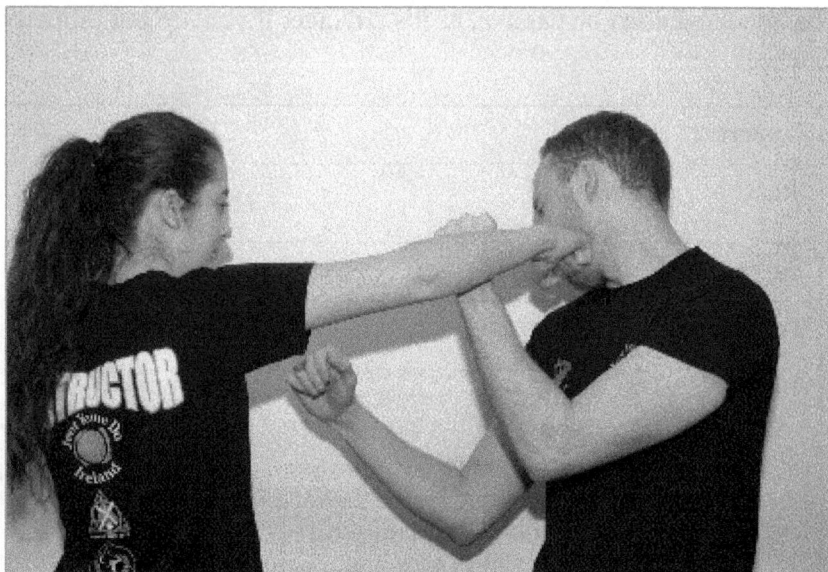

Olivia shoots an overhand punch bridging over the opponents guard

The overhand punch launches attack over the opponent's guard and requires excellent timing to get it just right. This unorthodox punch is very successful in UFC, leading to many knockouts.

Overhand punch	
Start	On guard
Target	Jaw or just behind the ear
Technique	1. Hands up 2. Chin down 3. Elbows in 4. Aim hand at target 5. Front hand makes a fist 6. Throw a looping arcing overhand punch 7. Snap punch as if throwing a ball 8. Hit through target 9. Snap back
Close	10. Return on guard 11. Hit focus pads to develop skill with a partner, swapping roles/sides

THE STRAIGHT BLAST

THE STRAIGHT BLAST

The straight blast is a turbo-charged JKD street survival technique designed to get things over in a few seconds. Learn it well as it could save your life. It's an unorthodox technique that requires diligent practice to get it right.

The straight blast	
Start	On guard
Target	Nose/jaw
Technique	1. On guard 2. Hands up 3. Chin down 4. Elbows tucked in 5. Aim at target 6. Imagine throwing a series of 10 jabs and crosses very fast to bulls eye on a dartboard 7. Punch at point of opponents nose/chin 8. Relax arms, shoulders 9. Strike with vertical fist straight to target 10. Use a "machine gun" rotation delivery 11. Snap back
Close	12. Return on guard 13. Hit focus pads or heavy bag in 10 second bursts, with partner 14. Swap roles/sides

The straight blast is a quick emergency technique for the JKD practitioner. As one fist punches, the other takes its place in an overhand rapid-fire attack sequence. This is a straight line, one hand hits, drops slightly allowing the next blow access. Aim right at the opponent's nose, bringing the hand back to centre before launching another punch. It returns in motion like a camshaft, attacking swiftly and efficiently.

This attack can completely overrun the opponent's defence, smashing him in the face as your weight comes in behind each blow.

Don't attack lightly with the hands, put proper body mechanics into each blow together with forward momentum. If stepping, use a short shuffle step rather than a running step as you can fall over the opponent's legs if he drops.

The straight blast needs to be used up-close and conservatively as it's very turbo-charged. It dramatically increases lactic acid in the arm muscles, leading to a quick burnout after a few seconds. Don't charge in like a bull in a china shop, blasting away aimlessly. Use this excellent technique purposefully, take aim and zap him with quick fire bursts.

HOW TO KEEP YOUR JKD POWDER DRY

In JKD there is a key principle of "non preparation and non-telegraphic motion" for all attacks.

This is considered vital for success. Many people tend load up their attacks and can be spotted before it is due to land. You'll also need to spend time training to erase the "tells" from your attack. Gaining the ability to recognise the signals of your opponent's attack will give you an advantage. Being just a fraction of a second ahead means that you are hitting first and upsetting his plans before he has a chance to hurt you.

LOWER BODY TECHNIQUES AND ACTIVATING THE BODY

As usual there are no short cuts to becoming proficient. You will need to make the effort and practice. Someone once said "the harder I practice, the better I get" and it is so very true. Things that will help develop fast efficient footwork are rope skipping and ladder running. There are several basic footwork methods used in JKD. These are described in short video clips at www.jkdireland.com.

STEP AND SLIDE

Step and slide footwork enables you to track an opponent, just staying out of range until you decide to attack or defend.

Step and slide	
Start	On guard
Target	Track opponent Keep correct fighting distance
Technique	1. On guard 2. Hands up 3. Elbows in 4. Knees slightly bent 5. 50/50 weight on each leg 6. Move forward 7. Take a half step forward with lead foot 8. Follow with a half step forward with the rear foot 9. Maintain on guard 10. Move back 11. Take a half step back with rear leg 12. Follow with half step back with front leg 13. Maintain on guard 14. Move feet and legs in sequence 15. Don't fall over!

This is a gravity-based pattern in which you can maintain the correct distance between you and your opponent. One foot moves forward or back and the other follows along while maintaining good form.

Note: The fighting measure is a half-step from the opponent

PUSH SHUFFLE

The push shuffle is essential in developing the ability to attack and defend with excellent mobility.

Push shuffle	
Start	1. On guard 2. Hands up 3. Chin down 4. Elbows in 5. Rear heel raised slightly 6. Front foot turned in a fraction 7. Knees slightly bent
Target	Maintaining fighting measure in attack/defence
Technique	1. Move forward 2. Push hard from the rear foot a half step 3. Front foot moves forward a half step at same time 4. Glide forward with the feet 5. Keep good balance and posture 6. Move back 7. Push back a half step with front leg 8. Rear leg moves back at the same time 9. Maintain excellent on guard posture

The push shuffle is used to propel the body forward or back to attack or retreat.

When done correctly it can place a great deal of power into your attack with the hands or feet. It's carried out by moving forward with the back "drive" leg, which employs the legs in a dynamic but controlled motion from the on guard position. Moving forward and back into the on guard position for several minutes at each workout is highly recommended. The push shuffle can be used to help you to retreat fast as well by pushing hard off the lead leg and driving back.

SIDE STEP

The ability to side step is important in evasion and setting up counter moves. Practice until it becomes second nature and move in a smooth motion.

Side step	
Start	On guard (right lead)
Target	Evasion and counter moves
Technique	1. On guard (to move left) 2. Hands up 3. Chin down 4. Elbows in 5. Start with right lead foot in front 6. Move left leg a quarter step to left 7. Move right leg a quarter step to left 8. Move head slightly to left 9. Maintain on guard 10. On guard (to move right) 11. Hands up 12. Chin down 13. Elbows in 14. Start right lead foot in front 15. Move right leg a quarter step to right 16. Move left leg a quarter step to right 17. Move head slightly to right 18. Keep good posture/balance

In the basic side step right lead, you may start by moving to your left. The left foot moves first followed by the right foot. At the same time, the head moves to the left to practice avoiding a head shot. The rear hand or protective hand also moves to the right to practice a parry.

When moving to the right, the right foot moves first followed by the left as the head moves to the right to avoid a head shot, the protective hand parries slightly to the left.

Now practice putting it all together by moving forward, backward, left and right. Please don't neglect this simple drill; practice and work in a left and right lead.

HALF PENDULUM

The half pendulum enables very fast attack sequences with kicks, which become hard to stop because of efficient movement and body mechanics.

Half pendulum footwork	
Start	On guard (right lead)
Target	Enable footwork attack and defence
Technique	1. On guard 2. Hands up 3. Elbows in 4. Chin down 5. 50/50 weight distribution 6. Moving forward 7. Tap rear left foot on right heel, shuffle forward a half step 8. Moving backward 9. Tap front right heel on rear foot, shuffle back a half step 10. Maintain good posture/balance 11. Return to On guard

Practice shadow sparring footwork using left and right on guard stances.

IDEAS ON TRAINING FOOTWORK

Good footwork is essential to your self-defence and enables you to move effectively and efficiently:

- O practice all the footwork drills in your training sessions
- O keep good posture and balance
- O maintain on guard at all times
- O the way to improve footwork is to practice it for a few minutes every time you workout and incorporate it into your activities.
- O practice hitting focus pads or use the mirror or partner and push shuffle to enter and retreat after each attack

KICKING

Kicking is an important aspect of JKD and many of the kicks we use are delivered below the waist to the knee and to the groin. This is because they are vulnerable areas and safer and easier to target than high line kicking.

Learn to kick well with both sides and with the lead leg and rear leg. Develop flexibility by regular stretching. Learn to use rhythm and employ good footwork to get in and out of range fluidly.

Incorporating excellent footwork is vital as kicks are slower than punches and can be telegraphed. But by using good footwork the kick can land efficiently and effectively.

Many but not all of the basic JKD kicks are delivered mainly with the front leg and then with the rear leg due to efficiency.

Tip: The fighting measure. Practice maintaining the fighting measure by keeping just a half step away from the opponent. This is an important idea in JKD and should be practiced regularly and considered.

HOOK KICK

Hook Kick (right kick with front leg)	
Start	On guard (right lead)
Target	Groin/ribs
Technique	1. Take a half step forward right foot followed by left foot 2. Place support foot at 45 degrees 3. Pivot foot away from kicking leg 4. Ensure good balance 5. Raise lead knee up facing target (note: leg follows the knee) 6. Raise lead hip 7. Raise thigh to parallel to floor and turn the hips over 8. Inner thigh should now be facing the floor 9. Arc to the target 10. Hit the groin/ribs with the instep or ball of the foot
Close	11. Return to on guard

Hook kick begins by make a half step (stutter step) with the front leg followed by the rear leg and raise the heel, knee and hips. Execute the kick at the target in a small arc motion. Ensure you're well balanced with hands up.

The kick uses the toe of the shoe, instep or ball of the foot to attack the groin or ribs. Delivery is usually off the front leg but use the rear leg as well. The French Savate hook kick is another favourite method with a swift arc snapping motion and using the toe of the (cowboy) boot into the ribs this is exquisitely painful.

LEAD LEG STOP/SHIN KICK

My mother used to say "kick him on the shins" and this is an actual JKD method which is very effective, if you're wearing hard shoes.

Execute the kick to the target and snap it back quickly, return efficiently to the on guard position. Stay mobile and react fast. It's a simple kick delivered with the side of the foot near the ankle. Target the knee/shin and it's very painful, this area has little muscle to protect it from damage. When wearing shoes or boots the foot becomes a more dangerous weapon.

Lead leg stop/shin kick	
Start	On guard
Target	Knee/shin
Technique	1. Hands up 2. Elbows in 3. Chin down 4. Take quick half step with lead leg 5. Take a quick half step with rear leg 6. Lead knee raises up slightly 7. Hip points at target 8. Pivot on supporting leg, heel faces target 9. Lead leg smashes downward through target 10. Return to on guard
Close	11. Use heavy leg guards to practice with partner or a standing heavy bag

In this stop kick, the foot is driven into the opponent's knee using the hip and forward motion. This is a very damaging manoeuvre.

Practice the kick to the target and snap it back quickly, return efficiently to the on guard position. Stay mobile and react fast.

JKD STRAIGHT KICK

This is a simple kick mainly delivered from the front leg. It can flick fast to the groin or be used more powerfully with the ball of the foot to the gut and driven forward with the hips and fast footwork.

Straight kick	
Start	On guard
Target	Groin or abdomen
Technique	1. On guard 2. Hands up 3. Chin down 4. Take a half step forward with front leg 5. Take a half step behind with rear leg 6. Place support foot at 45 degree angle 7. Ensure good balance 8. Raise knee up 9. Don't lock knees 10. Snap kick swiftly to groin 11. Or thrust kick to midsection 12. Hit target with instep or ball of foot, snap kick back 13. Keep hands up
Close	14. Return to on guard 15. Use focus pads with a partner 16. Swap sides /roles

Straight kick travels from the on guard position to hit the opponents knee or groin in a fast snapping motion. It can also be used to attack the midsection thrusting the ball of the foot.

This kick, when wearing shoes, can be used to kick the shin/knee with the tip of the shoe or boot making it a very painful weapon.

JKD SIDE KICK

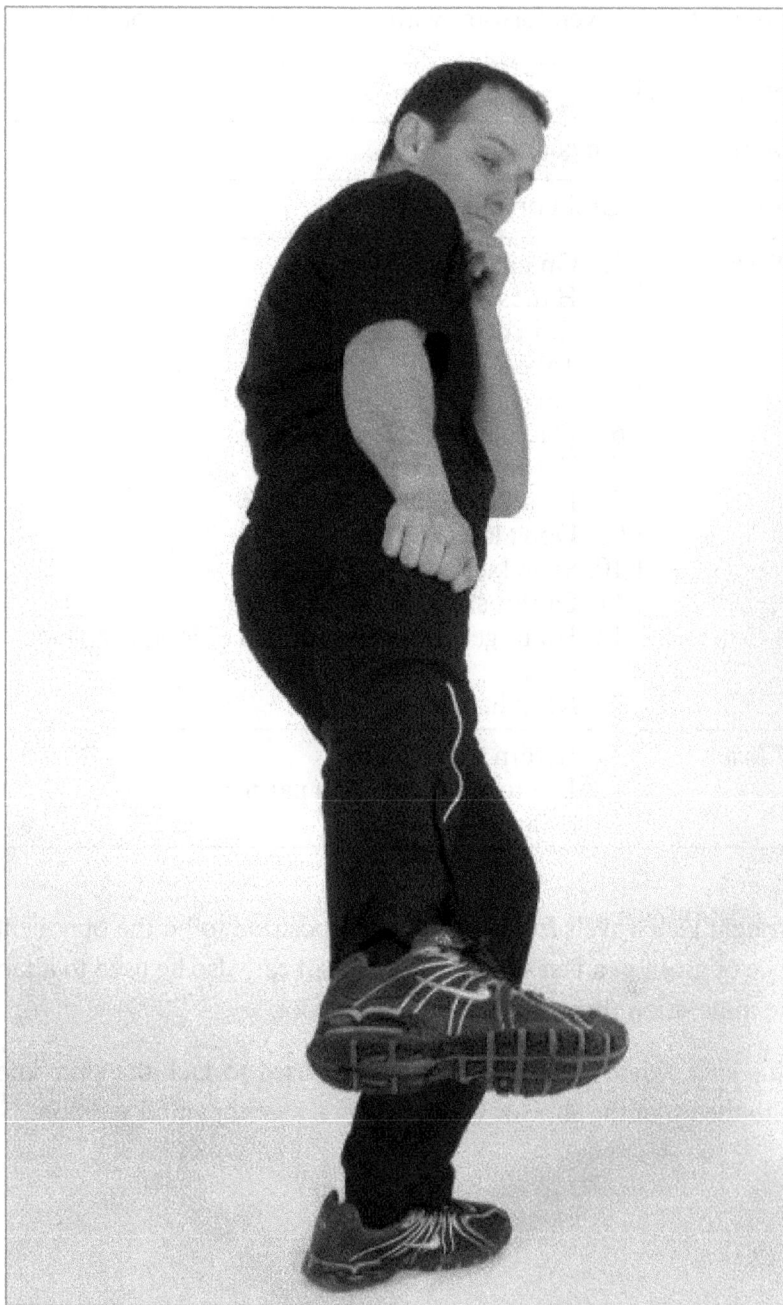

The side kick is a powerful kick but can be telegraphed and caught if not employed properly. The image shows a low side kick.

Side kick	
Start	On guard (right lead)
Target	Midsection
Technique	1. On guard 2. Hands up 3. Chin down 4. Take a half step forward with right front leg 5. Step behind lead leg with rear leg 6. Pivot on rear standing leg, heel faces same way as kicking direction 7. 70% of weight shifts to rear leg 8. Raise knee up 9. Raise hip, bring right heel and knee up to same level, parallel to floor facing target 10. Turn hips 11. Ensure good balance 12. "Sit behind the kick", don't lean back 13. Thrust hips and leg through target using side of foot
Close	14. Return to on guard 15. Use kick shield with a partner and swap sides / roles

To begin a side kick take a small step with the front foot followed by a step behind and thrust the lead leg through the target. Ensure hips are open and "sit" behind the kick, don't lean far back.

Work with a partner and a kick shield to get the feel for this kick. Kick it lightly to get a feel for the kick and then increase to full power.

The side kick is a power blow and thrusts forward into the attack with a mighty force. It is often used with the fast step footwork to gain more power and superior use of distance, crashing in very quickly. However it mustn't be telegraphed. If used improperly, kicks can be caught and grapplers can take swift advantage, dumping you on the ground and finishing you quickly.

THAI BOXING ROUND KICK

Thai boxing right round kick	
Start	On guard (a slightly wider stance than usual)
Target	Thigh/ribs
Technique	1. On guard (left leg leading) 2. Hands up 3. Chin down 4. Have support foot at about a 45 degree angle 5. Ensure good balance 6. Turn hip, raise knee and swing rear leg, chopping through target 7. Pivot well on ball of supporting foot, heel facing direction of kick 8. Fully torque hips into kick 9. Strike with shin to outside of opponent's leg/ribs, follow through with hip 10. Imagine a baseball bat swing movement, hit right through the target and don't pull back 11. Hands up
Close	12. Return on guard 13. Use Thai pads or heavy bag swap partner/roles

The Thai boxing roundhouse kick is quite devastating. Imagine delivering this kick as similar to swinging an axe at a tree, or baseball bat, hitting with the shin bone onto the outside of the opponent's leg muscle or ribs.

HEEL HOOK KICK 180 DEGREES

This kick is good for balance and technical excellence but is not recommended for the street as it can leave you vulnerable to being dumped on the ground by a grappler/ streetfighter.

Sweep kick (180 degree reverse roundhouse)	
Start	On guard
Target	Ribs/jaw/temple
Technique	1. On guard 2. Hands up 3. Elbows in 4. Chin down 5. Take a half step forward with right lead kicking leg 6. Rear leg steps behind the lead leg 7. Raise hip 8. Raise knee 9. Inner thigh parallel to floor 10. Launch kick in clockwise sweeping upward arc to target 11. Strike with the heel to the jawline 12. Keep balanced
Close	13. Return to on guard 14. Use focus pads/heavy bag 15. Swap roles/sides

SPIN BACK KICK

Spin back kick is a counter-offensive one which can catch a rushing opponent.

Spin back kick	
Start	On guard
Target	Ribs/midsection
Technique	1. On guard (left lead) 2. Hands up 3. Elbows in 4. Chin down 5. Feint a lead hand jab or finger jab 6. Spin and pivot on support leg 7. Heel facing target 8. Spin around, keep balance 9. Look quickly over your shoulder at target 10. Thrust rear leg through target 11. Strike with heel toes pointing down
Close	12. Return to on guard 13. Use kick shield to practice kick with a partner 14. Swap roles/sides

KNEE SPIKE

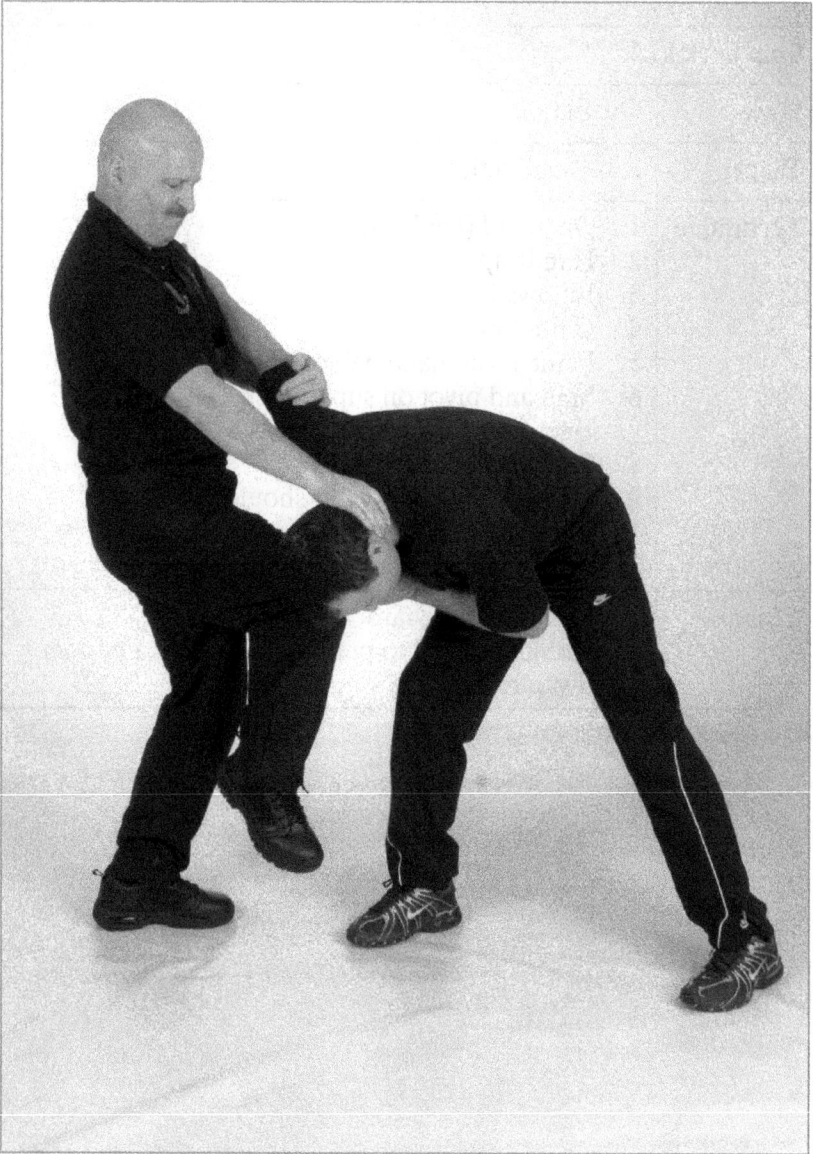

The knee spike is a useful technique for a close-range headshot or to "crush nuts". Drive a lead or rear knee into the attacker's groin or femoral nerve.

Use full bodyweight and drive it forward hard with the point of the knee impacting. Here, the opponent's arm is grabbed and knee driven to the head.

Knee spike	
Start	On guard
Target	Groin/femoral nerve
Technique	1. On guard 2. Hands up 3. Elbows in 4. Chin down 5. Drive rear knee forward into target 6. Point of knee impacting 7. Use full body weight 8. Keep hands up protect face 9. Lean back slightly 10. Use left and right leg
Close	11. Return on guard 12. Use Thai Pads or heavy bag 13. swap roles / swap sides

By grabbing and holding onto the opponent's neck or jacket a quick blast of knees in succession can be devastating. This gives an opponent a concussion, dead leg or squashed nuts, ouch! Beware of getting your leg caught by a grappler so be super-fast in delivery on low line.

GUIDELINES FOR KICKING

Learning to kick well allows you to dictate an encounter, attacking at long range. A well-aimed kick is more powerful than a punch. It is a primary weapon in attack and low-line kicks are difficult to stop.

Kicking progression methods

As you have seen, kicking adds a brilliant exciting dimension to your workouts.

Everyone likes to kick well but this requires lots of practice. Do each kick 20 times and build up to 100 repetitions. Soon you will have 1,000 repetitions and start to own the techniques for yourself. When training for progression, include some of the following techniques to add variety to your workouts.

There are short video clips at: www.jkdireland.com.

- hook kick
- straight kick
- side kick,
- back kick
- oblique kick
- 180 degree kick
- 360 degree kick

HOW NOT TO GET YOUR ASS HANDED TO YOU

Sloppy kicking and high kicks in the street are more than likely to get you beaten up in the process. Don't engage in a kicking fest on the street with some idiot as it's just plain ridiculous unless you are a top UFC fight athlete or the Champion Kicker of the World.

You may think that your kicks are great in the gym but on the street they won't deliver the goods unless you are really good, smart and extra sneaky.

Kicks get caught and stuffed so you may swiftly end up on the ground eating pavement and goodness knows what else. They also look ridiculous if your flailing about acting the kung fu king. So my advice is to keep any kicks to a bare minimum and at knee or groin level.

KICKING MASTERY

Good technique reduces the risk of injury. There are some tips for kicking:

1. start with on guard – kicking well is more challenging than punching

2. keep well balanced

3. work on flexibility regularly

4. start slowly, feel the technique

5. avoid locking the knee

6. raise the knee parallel to the floor as you kick

7. raise the hip

8. don't fling the leg

9. don't telegraph kicks

10. keep knees slightly bent

11. be efficient and effective

12. finish on guard

SECTION 5

SPARRING AND FIGHTING

"The only place that success comes before
work is in the dictionary"
Vince Lombardi

SPARRING AND FIGHTING

Technical sparring is when two people move around throwing punches and kicks at one another without intending to really hurt their opponent. In training, partners often tacitly agree to go about 50% power.

SPARRING AS A BROWN BELT

When I was a karate brown belt, I was asked by a tough professional boxer if I would like to spar? Of course I agreed, thinking I was a tough guy too.

But this guy had fought the World Light Middleweight champion Ayub Kalule and so hit me very hard for a few rounds.

It taught me something I have never forgotten – respect for boxing. That was another reality check for me. Thank you Ray for knocking some sense into me.

Sparring doesn't teach a person how to finish a fight quickly. So instead of doing too much, include in your sessions slamming a lot of nasty, open-hand techniques, headbutts, knees and elbows on a well-padded partner.

Use focus mitts and big kick shields, hitting in a few explosive seconds. That is three, five or ten seconds maximum. You will be surprised at how quickly you gas out and become exhausted. Get your breath back and repeat this many times and use it to simulate a mass attack with a group as well.

Repeat the cycle regularly and you'll develop your nasty fighting skills and technique very quickly.

If you spar – and you should do some – it's important to do it progressively. As a beginner, don't go all out to spar with experienced people until you know how to handle yourself with basic technique. Always keep your guard up and learn to defend well.

Don't go out to bash each other when sparring, use it as a learning tool to build your basics. See what works for you and how you react. In the beginning you will make lots of mistakes but you'll improve as you progress.

Your sparring sessions need to be tailored to you as an individual as we are all built differently and have likes and dislikes. Some are tall or short, some are less or more aggressive and so on.

Use a two or three-minute round at the start and rotate the sparring partners if possible. Ensure a reasonable match up as beginners can get hurt if this isn't done. I like to put a beginner with a more experienced person to show them the ropes. Make sure that you have the proper sparring equipment – mouth guard, 16oz gloves, leg guards, headgear.

In the beginning use as much protective gear as you wish. Then, as you gain confidence, you will want to use less as it can hamper your movement.

DON'T DO WHAT I DID

Some head cases in sparring were really trying to hurt me and bash me hard. I usually tried my hardest to retaliate as the red mist descended.

But one of these tough guys kicked me so hard that I lost several teeth and was knocked clean out. I couldn't remember a thing when I woke up.

That was a long time ago and I didn't know there were mouth guards for sale in the shop.

Naturally, because I'm an idiot, I refused to go to hospital and lay in bed for a day with a pounding headache. The dentist bill cost me a week's salary.

I had neglected to check in advance with my instructor – or the guy's psychiatrist – what type of sparring we were doing. Him being a bit of a lad, he just wanted to batter me anyway.

I was just back from months working away and stood there like an idiot in front of him with no guard. There are differences in sparring so make sure you are fully appraised as to what type you're engaging in.

When sparring wear a mouth guard, keep your chin down, keep your hands up and be ready.

ISOLATION TECHNICAL SPARRING

The idea of isolation sparring is to improve technical efficiency while building confidence and competence in a fairly minimum-stress environment. This does introduce some stress but should be an enjoyable learning experience. The practitioner gets to try out various techniques and game plans to dominate.

Firstly, put on plenty of protective equipment and familiarise yourself with it as it becomes second nature. The idea is to gradually increase the tempo and pressure over time while having an intensive learning experience and enjoyable training session.

Hard sparring should really only take place between more experienced and hard core students. Beginners get put off, hurt and discouraged by the intimidating atmosphere created.

Most people come into martial arts because they lack confidence or are in need of help and support, not to be used as punching bags for higher ranks.

PROGRESSION IDEAS FOR TECHNICAL SPARRING

- ○ front hand v front hand (punches versus punches)
- ○ front foot v front foot (kicks vs kicks)
- ○ two hands v two hands (punching with both hands)
- ○ two feet v two feet (kicking with either leg)
- ○ grappler v boxer (one guy acts as a grappler vs an opponent who can only box)
- ○ grappler v kicker
- ○ grappler v grappler (start standing or on knees on the ground)

Throw a training dagger into the mix and you have a very different dynamic. It's interesting to observe the reaction of guys grappling on the ground, when you throw in a training dagger. All the fancy moves go out the window very quickly as blind panic sets in.

Any mix of the above will give lots of experiences, as will all-out sparring for the more experienced practitioners. Remember that sparring is not "real fighting" and keep it in perspective. Your sparring partner is not trying to kill you.

TRAPPING

Trapping is the temporary immobilisation of a limb, leg or body to give you an opportunity to control or bash an attacker without them being able to hit you back. For example if you punch and he blocks it, this clash may give you an opportunity to quickly execute a slap hit to his jaw, throat or nose.

But you shouldn't go looking for a trap unless you are highly skilled as it can lead you into trouble. Keep it simple and direct. Successful trapping takes a lot of time and effort. If you have the inclination to put in the time to develop the skills, then go for it.

Here are some basic trapping sequences. There are short video clips at: www.jkdireland.com.

SLAP HIT – PAK SAO

In this technique you drive the opponent's arm back towards them with your rear hand as you then crash in and hit with your lead hand.

GRAB AND HIT – LOP SAO

Imagine grabbing the opponent's arm by the wrist, pulling his arm towards your waist sharply and at the same time striking him on the jaw

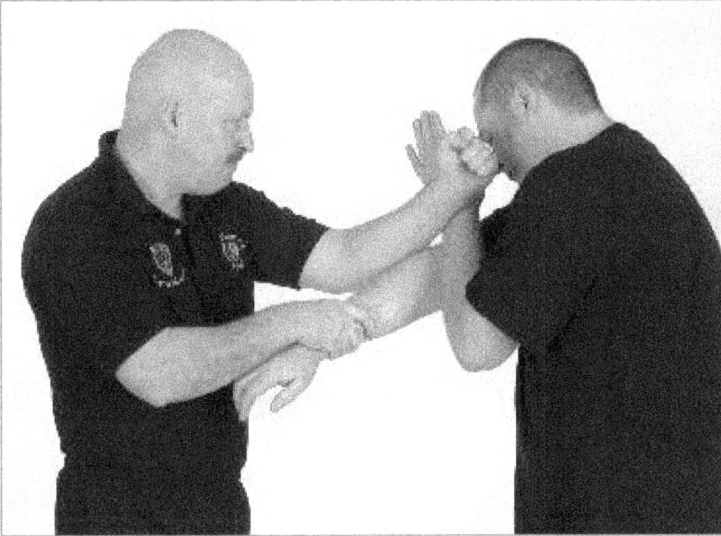

CROSS GRAB AND HIT – LIN LOP SAO

Use this technique if the opponent blocks your initial attack. Pull his arm across his body and strike.

MY FIRST FULL CONTACT FIGHT

It was 1978 and this was the new craze coming from the USA. I trained twice a day for 12 weeks for a four-round fight and worked out with a team of tough boxers and bouncers.

I was in the best condition of my life, super fit and the sparring was very hard. I got knocked down a few times and jumped back in straight away.

On the night, my more experienced opponent got the fight changed to two rounds, which threw me off balance. I trained for a longer battle and did not change my tactics, so I lost before it even started.

He went all-out in the first round and narrowly won. I started to hurt him in the second, but he used his ring experience to cling to me like a limpet and stifle me – I couldn't shake the bugger off. He won but I knew that if the fight had gone on longer I would have beaten him as he was gassing out.

Another lesson learned, expect the unexpected and be prepared to change tactics in an instant. Don't think about fighting in rounds get it over fast .

THE FOUR QUADRANTS FOR DEFENCE

In JKD, the hands are used to protect the upper body above the waist and the legs to protect the lower body.

The rear hand is mostly used to defend the upper four quadrants or gates:

- ○ imagine the body divided in half by a line at hip height and another straight line running from the top of the head and nose to groin
- ○ use mostly the rear hand to protect these four upper body quadrants
- ○ imagine that you are standing in a rectangular box and your hands can't move to much beyond your body to block any blows
- ○ this idea keeps your defensive actions to a bare minimum and you don't waste time on blocking

1. Outside high parry with punch

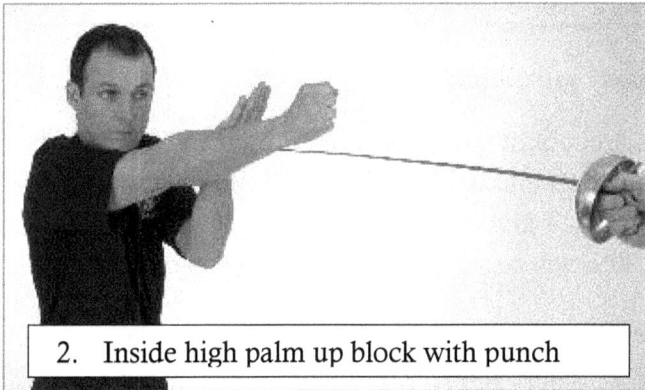

2. Inside high palm up block with punch

3. Outside low block with punch

4. Inside low block with punch

Lower body protection

The legs and use of good footwork protect the lower body, because it makes no sense to use the hands for this. For example if you bend over to block a kick you may receive a knee in the face for your trouble. This will be further explained in the supporting videos.

Interception

The highest skill in JKD is to intercept the opponent on his intention, preparation, delivery or recovery of his attack.

Each of these skills are challenging and require much practice. Counter-attacking must be carried out like a bolt of lightning.

Evasion

In JKD it's best to be a matador, not a bull. Remember that the opponent is trying to hit you so it's important to evade the attacks as a priority. Develop skills to avoid them and minimise possible damage to you.

JKD emphasises proper stance and mobility, keeping just a half step away is vital in avoiding attacks. Learn how to avoid and slip punches, and parry or block attacks, move your head out of the way and quickly counterattack.

Blocking

Learn how to block attacks and to safely absorb punches that cannot be evaded and avoided. To achieve skills in blocking there is a need to have a well-conditioned body and a strong stance.

For example, guard your face and head with your hands and use your forearms and shins to absorb strikes that cannot be avoided. Let the punch come towards you and cover, don't chase after it intercept it. Hard blocking is least favoured in JKD, however you need to know how to do it well especially against a very aggressive fighter. Using fancy or weak blocks against a good fighter will get you hurt or knocked out.

SECTION 6

STREET SMARTS

"People should learn to see and so avoid danger. Just as a wise man keeps away from mad dogs, so one should not make friends with evil men."
Buddha

STREET SMARTS

This is the right down and dirty section. It contains key information and sound advice on street self-protection, including how to handle aggression and violence should it come your way and how to spot it coming.

WOOFING – KNOW YOUR ENEMY

Rory Miller says that street attacks may begin with a pre-interview such as "woofing". Woofing is someone talking trash at you, cursing you and winding you up by calling you names or insulting you big time. They are testing you out to see how you react and if you react badly they may attack you.

Bare this in mind and take heed of the following:

- watch your body language
- be mindful, in control and exude a strong and calm confidence, but don't be cocky
- keep any reaction as simple as possible
- if you can talk you way out of trouble then do so
- always try to anticipate an attack at long range and don't be in the danger zone in the first place
- if you are in danger, get away as quickly if possible
- don't get into a drunken argument or fight on the street as people get maimed or killed doing this

HOW ATTACKS CAN BEGIN

AN AMBUSH

This is pre-planned on the attacker's side and you make the mistake of walking into or across a choke point whereby you get distracted by one person and are then sucker-punched and mugged by another or by several attackers.

A choke point may be an intersection on a street, at a cash point or a shortcut where attackers can wait, prepared for their victim.

If this happens to you may be able to use one of the following options

1. Run away, which is a very good option
2. Fight them for your glory and ego, which is generally a very stupid idea and can get you badly hurt or killed
3. Give them your wallet, credit card and hope that they don't beat you up and exit quickly. Consider throwing your money and/or wallet on the ground or at them to catch and run like hell. Possibly carry two wallets, one with an out-of-date credit card and some cash and hand it over. This is probably a smart move.

If someone pulls a knife on you the main question you need to ask yourself is how much do you value your life?

Is you cash or wallet worth more than being maimed, scarred for life, possibly brain damaged or even killed? If you get stabbed in the gut, you may end up having to wear a colostomy bag for life. It's not worth risking.

ROBBERY AT KNIFE POINT

Imagine you are at a cash point late at night. Someone behind you pulls a knife on you and demands money.

You feel confident as you have been to a knife self defence class. You try to block the knife but mistime it when the attacker swings at you. You get cut and badly injured as a result and repairing the scars costs thousands of pounds.

Would you have been safer just handing over the money? What do you think about this scenario?

THE ART OF FIGHTING WITHOUT FIGHTING

Imagine that something bad happens in a club, pub or crowded place. Someone starts staring at you, swearing and raising their voice. They're getting wide-eyed and arms splayed, and shouting, "What the f**k are you looking at?".

If you see them shifting their stance and weight, be ready and prepared as they are going to attack.

You may notice a body jerk just as they are about to launch an attack which is an adrenaline dump into their system.

You need to have both your hands up right in front of your face at an angle of about 90 degrees, with open palms facing the person and not in balled fists. Tuck your elbows in to the sides.

First, if you can, say to the person in a firm and clear voice so that others can hear you, "I don't want any trouble." But be prepared for an attack, which could be a wide swing usually with the right hand (your left side) or a headbutt, or perhaps a sneaky beer glass attack.

If the attack is happening it's vital that you don't wait. You need to strike before he does and "attack into the attack" hard agressively and fast. The longer you wait, the more chance you have of being hurt.

If he grabs your jacket and starts to punch, you have to get your counter-attack in quickly. The key is not to wait even if he is much bigger and stronger, you must attack him as hard as you can.

If attacked you can use reasonable force against them to defend yourself. Then just get away to a safe place as fast as you can.

WINNING

It's your responsibility to keep yourself and your loved ones safe and secure. There is no 100% safe solution to an attack and the main objective for you is to survive by not fighting if possible. However, winning is always best option if it kicks off. Fight or flight options will depend on circumstances and your assessment, which may have to change in an instant.

- If the attack is imminent, end it as soon as possible because the longer it goes on the more dangerous it becomes.
- If he hits you, hit him back harder
- Don't make silly mistakes.
- Keep it simple
- Finish it in seconds, not minutes as you'll quickly become exhausted due to stress and adrenaline flooding your body.

Your mind is your greatest weapon, but you've got to be healthy, fit and strong as well. There's no such thing as a fair fight now days, so use anything at hand to survive and live to tell the tale.

TROUNCING YOUR ENEMIES

The point to stress here is that there are no tricks or shortcuts to defeating your enemies. You need to train in the basics and learn them well, and be in very good physical shape. Employ speed, surprise and violence of action.

Finish the fight before he realises he's in one and get it over quickly. You can then walk into your home in one piece.

Fancy moves look great in the movies or demonstrations against a cooperative partner. But in a real scrap against a ruthless, determined enemy you will gas out quickly and could get you badly injured or killed.

PRESSURE TESTING

By placing yourself in difficult situations while training you will learn the difference between hitting the bag or pads and having a reality check. In a difficult contest or hard sparring match, your brilliant techniques may not work so well or not at all. It's also important to develop strong skills in handling a takedown or tackle attempt.

Learn how to control your emotions in a disciplined way by placing yourself in uncomfortable positions. Clear your mind and do your best. Great athletes say that they have tunnel vision when they are under pressure. This means that they are controlling their emotions and fear through concentration and preparation. In our training methods each person is taught the basic techniques in the same way but each individual will express these slightly differently.

IMPOSE YOUR WILL

The great boxing trainer Cus D'Amato said that in a contest it's a matter of one fighter imposing his will on the other. He trained his fighters all the same way – including world champions Mike Tyson and Floyd Patterson – but they all expressed this differently in the ring.

It's said that great fighters have a high degree of aggression in them to maintain the very difficult training regime and endure the hard sparring fights and beatings. Many people can't understand this and don't put themselves under any pressure and give up too easily in a contest. Remember that life is a contest, so don't give up and stay physically fit.

SOME GOOD MOVES

JKD is good for self-defence because at its core it's simple, direct and effective. It's easy to learn the basics and remember them in hours, not months or years. It's not just about developing the ability to knock someone out, even though that may be necessary at some point. It's more than that. Using a JKD mindset can help you become fitter, stronger, and lose fat while building lean muscle.

It's pretty useless learning a self defence system or martial art that takes years to master – and even worse or fatal to discover it won't work under pressure.

After many decades of practice and research it's clear to me that all martial arts are valuable. However many work best against someone from the same background or style. Problems arise if and when a young fit very aggressive street fighter is pitted against a stylist who is unused to extremely violent, wild, unpredictable and random attacks.

Try mixing training sessions with a totally uncooperative partner who is resisting your techniques. This is one of the reasons that skilled martial artists may get beaten up in the street.

JKD is designed to work in the real world and the basics are effective and take minimal maintenance. For instance how much time does it take to learn a finger jab to the eye, or headbutt, elbow to the jaw and knee to the groin. Not much. However you must be in good physical condition as well, so neglect this at your peril.

LEARN TO FIGHT ON THE GROUND

It's important to be able to fight in all ranges with or without a weapon, including on the ground. For example, in an altercation you may fall over, get tripped up, hit from behind or tackled on the blind-side. Familiarise yourself with excellent takedown defence, ground-fighting tactics and techniques.

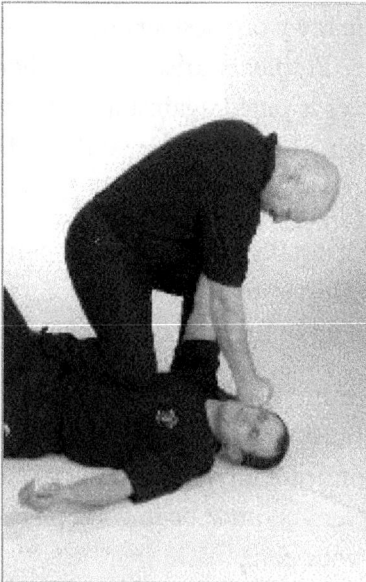

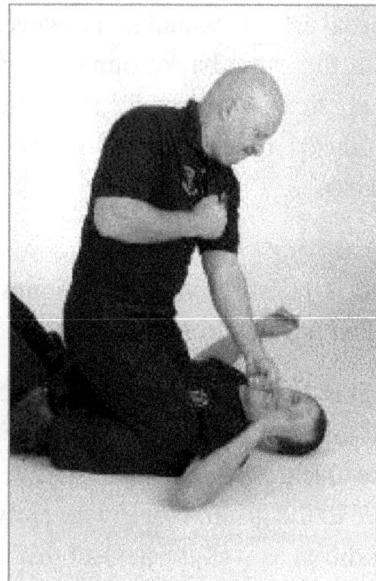

Develop the ability to get up quickly from a bad situation from your back. Try it and you will find that it's not so easy. Don't think about a submission or tapping him out on the street, gouge or break something and get back up fast.

Remember that grappling will exhaust you extremely quickly so get some good experience and conditioning. Learn the basics from a good grappling or Brazilian Jiu Jitsu coach. It's estimated that grappling may burn almost 900 calories an hour as it is so intense.

It's really wonderful for mobility and conditioning. Teaching tactics on how to control a bigger stronger resisting opponent is also important. Don't be in denial as some day you may have to fight for your life from the ground.

The following are a few simple techniques to avoid being taken to the ground:

Your attacker comes at you low with both arms trying to get behind your knees for a "double leg tackle":

Strategy 1	1. Sprawl with both of your legs back fast to prevent him from getting his grips in on the back of your legs and place both your hands onto his shoulders and push very hard downwards, he will eat the sidewalk. 2. Keep your legs well back to avoid him grabbing on and push him down hard.
Strategy 2	As he comes in to tackle, slam an arm very hard on his neck area and use the other to palm strike or claw his face and or eyes. Then push him swiftly to the ground.
Strategy 3	As he comes crashing in, hit him hard on the sides of his neck with both elbows. Bang him hard on the lower sides of his neck and drive him to the ground.

If the attacker puts an arm around your neck from behind to choke you:

Strategy	1. Use your two hands to quickly pull his arm down hard as you bend forward. 2. Twist to the side to escape .

In a guillotine choke from the front, the attacker has your head inside his arm at the side:

Strategy	1. Pull down on his arm with one hand and make space. 2. Slam groin strikes in very hard with your other hand to free yourself.

In a headlock from the side, the attacker is holding your head under his arm:

Strategy	1. Grab/trap his free arm with yours so he can't punch you in the face.
	2. Push upward, standing tall as you pull on his headlock attack arm and duck behind him.
	3. Push him away or into a wall/ table.

Hit them in the brainbox:

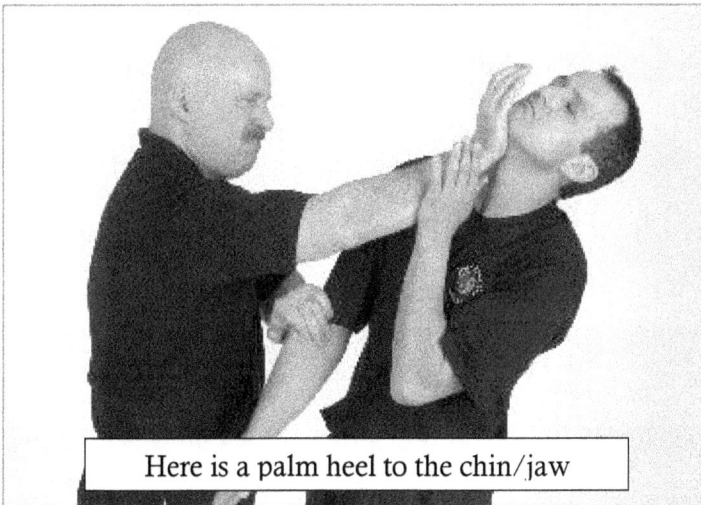

Here is a palm heel to the chin/jaw

Don't hit your opponent on the chest, back or shoulders as he won't feel it. You have to target vulnerable areas such as eyes, jaw, throat, groin. These are all good attack targets, however you must use the right tool for the job.

Remember: If all you have is a hammer you will treat everything as a nail.

Select the right tool for the job and disrupt their computer centre, the brain. Once the brain is stunned or they are made unconscious, their body cannot function for a moment and that is when you escape.

MY FIRST NIGHT AS A BOUNCER

The first time I worked as a bouncer I got involved in a serious melee. There were about a dozen of these guys and they outnumbered me and my fellow doormen about three to one.

At one stage I jumped across the crowd of fighting men and did a leaping flying "Superman punch". It came much to the surprise of my opponent and the bouncers, who later laughed their ass off at my crazy stupid technique.

I would have been better sticking to the basics.

BITING AND FIGHTING

Biting is much more frequent nowadays and can leave very bad facial injuries, so don't let anyone bite you – and if they do, don't pull away.

Keeping pressure on their jawline stops them from biting. Put your head against their jaw and put on pressure with a "Bulgarian Skull Crusher". Don't let their face to get into your space and allow them freedom to bite you. Control the head. Remember where the head moves the body will follow.

If your opponent is biting you, stick your thumb(s) deep and hard into his eye socket and keep the pressure right there until he releases. Only when he releases do you push him away and get out of there fast.

Be careful because their friends and partners may kick off and attack you. Don't wait around for a post mortem as it could be yours.

HOW TO DEFEND IN A CRISIS AND AVOID GOING TO JAIL

In learning how to defend yourself and your loved ones, remember this one thing: It's important that a reaction to an attack doesn't result in you going to prison. Any response you make has to be justified, using reasonable force.

Situations are different. For instance, imagine your reaction to a man breaking into your house. In some countries you could possibly have the legal right to take this man's life. In others you don't and will go to jail if you do.

Imagine the actions taken in defending your home against a burglar. In the first, on being discovered the burglar runs away and you ring the police. In the second, you chase the burglar down the street, catch him and beat him with a bat. One will result in no police action against you and the other may end up with you going to prison.

If you find yourself in an altercation and the police interview you, don't blurt out the first thing in your head as you may regret it in court. Saying, "I thought that he was going to hit me so I filled him in just in case officer" is not a good idea.

Try, "I was very afraid. I asked him to stop and he hit me. I was defending myself" or "Officer I was afraid for my life, I thought that I was in great danger".

The police will be writing down what you say, so be careful and allow yourself some time to calm down and think.

AFTER A FIGHT

In the aftermath of a street fight, the police will assume that both parties are guilty and willingly participated in the altercation. Your opponent will lie and tell the police that you started the assault, even if you didn't, and that you are the guilty party.

Remember, it's best not to get involved in fighting in the first place unless there is no other option, as fighting assumes that both parties are willing participants and both are equally guilty of assault, GBH or similar offences.

In a crisis, being trained will help you to react fast mentally and physically. This is vital in an emergency. However, good and bad choices are always possible.

For instance, imagine that your opponent has already decided to attack. He is several steps ahead in the decision making process. In his short-term business plan you are the prize and his objective is to take you down, destroy you and take what he wants.

In an emergency, I advocate not engaging with your opponent, but disengaging them with shock to turn the tables and survive.

AN ATTACKER WOULD NEVER DO THAT, OR WOULD HE

Noted author Loren W Christensen wrote an article in Palladin Press on sloppy defensive tactics and thinking. He critiqued the way that some instructors think that attackers will come at a person in a pre-set manner.

This is far from the case and this type of thinking can get a person seriously injured or killed. Muggers will get in a sneaky sucker punch, kick or stab and slash to rob and rape as easily as possible. They have no moral code or compass and view the public as sheep and themselves as wolves.

Instructors who think that choreographed and pre-set katas, training and techniques give real world success are generally kidding themselves and giving dangerous messages to their students. They need to get out more and educate themselves.

Note the YouTube video by Jim Carrey on knife defence. In this video Carrey gives a hilarious self-defence course to women which debunks pre-set training methods:
https://youtu.be/h_vvI26NnwE

DON'T TRY PUTTING FANCY MOVES OR LOCKS ON A DRUNK OR DRUGGED PERSON

Be wary of trying to wrestle or tap someone out as if they are drunk or drugged or both. They will have a high pain threshold and won't feel normal pain.

Tapping someone out is for competition and a street attack is not a sparring match. If attacked, hitting with open palms is very good, hit on jawline and groin and keep hitting until the person is subdued.

FEAR AND TERROR SAFETY TIPS

Terror attacks and fear of them are becoming more commonplace even though they are unlikely. It's wise to take some simple precautions when out and about. For example, when entering a mall or shopping centre take a mental note of the fire exits and sit near one if possible. In a cafe or bar sit facing the doorway to see who's coming and going. In an emergency you need to get out fast.

If a smoke alarm goes off or fire breaks out leave quickly. If in the very unlikely event that an attack is launched by someone with a knife or a gunman and you can't get out fast, go to the most secure room that you can find and barricade the doors with furniture or anything that you can find. Get behind steel filing cabinets and anything strong and sturdy. Look for makeshift weapons, use your imagination.

A really good makeshift weapon is a powder fire extinguisher, activate it right in the face of an attacker. Or it could be a chair with the legs pointing at an attacker, a broom handle, even running round a desk or table to stay away like the "Three Stooges" or throwing anything to hand at an attacker.

Learn some simple practical defence techniques. Don't be a passive victim and fight back if and when you can with ferocity. The FBI

---

statistics on people fighting back against an attacker, prove that fighting hard greatly improves the chances of survival.

Work together in a group to overpower an attacker if possible and overwhelm them with sheer force of numbers. Attackers depend on keeping you frozen with fear. When you break this blind panic state, you'll have a better chance to survive.

If the attacker's motive is a sexual assault or rape, then fighting back is a primary option. The FBI reports that women who fight back survive more than those who don't.

SECTION 7

BEING A HAPPY WARRIOR

"A sound mind in a sound body"
Juvenal

BEING A HAPPY WARRIOR

Throughout this book you will have seen that taking small positive steps every day you can make practical, real achievements. You can see that keeping going through difficult times and hard challenges is possible. There is no magic formula involved, just make a realistic plan and stick to it daily.

HOW TO KEEP GOING

Keep it going with small achievable steps every week and month. Give yourself a pat on the back and a small reward for reaching your goals.

FIGHTING SPIRIT

One of the themes that you will notice in this book is that life has often knocked me down and sideways too. What matters is that I have got back up and started again.

Sometimes I wonder if this is just plain stupidity, me being stubborn, or fighting spirit. My family and friends think it's a genetic thing, as I come from a long line of idiots who refused to give up fighting. Coming back from a heart attack that nearly killed me raised my fighting spirit.

"BEGRUDGERY"

This has a long tradition in Ireland and elsewhere. Just when you're getting somewhere good some dirty rotter will delight in pulling you back down.

"Don't let the b******s get you down," is a great motto. Be strong and determined, break the chains and have courage. Think to yourself, "This is hard but I can do it" – and you can.

MAKE SMALL CHANGES, DON'T TAKE ON TOO MUCH

Making small changes at the start is a great way to succeed. Trying to do too much will make it seem too hard and you may become bored or frustrated.

If you are training for an event and shut yourself away day-in, day-out without socialising you will become lonely, isolated and depressed. Snap out of that mindset and aim for a more balanced lifestyle.

AVOID GOING TO FAST TOO QUICKLY

If you try to go too fast you run the risk of injury or burnout. Remember to pace yourself, especially in the beginning as your body needs time to adjust to the training and lifestyle changes.

Build the changes up gradually and they will last longer.

My advice is to avoid hard as nails coaches who are pushing you super-tough from the start, unless perhaps you have what it takes to be a world champion fighter. Some coaches appear to have huge egos and are very proud of making students suffer. Good coaches lift people up not put them down or humiliate them.

REFLECT ON TRAINING BENEFITS

The benefits of training include improved mental health and physical wellbeing, and increased confidence and physical appearance. Overcoming obstacles and keeping going is important in mastering a JKD mindset and techniques. Sometimes it's good to be persistent and stubborn.

Proving something to oneself and others can be a motivational. Giving and receiving positive feedback and praise is very important as it helps to develop confidence, self-belief and self-esteem.

BOOST YOUR OVERALL WELLBEING

The emotional and physical rewards from JKD and training are really great. Taking charge of your health, wellbeing and fitness, and seeing your body change shape gives a real sense of empowerment. This in turn leads to enhanced motivation to keep healthy and fit and to reach for new and diverse goals. I often find that happy people are generally healthy people.

There is a link between a positive mindset and good physical wellbeing. It's known that too much stress is bad for your health but it's how you cope with stress is what's really important. When I worked in a factory making garbage cans, I would never have dreamed of becoming a JKD instructor or earning an honours degree. The process has taken a long time plus plenty of endurance, but the journey has been an exciting and rewarding one.

CARDIO AND BODY COMPOSITION BENEFITS

It's important to note what intensive JKD training can do for your body and fitness. It burns fat, which is the biggest store of fuel for the body and is used 24/7 for normal functions such as keeping warm, breathing digestion. The body burns fat while sleeping and sitting. (Romjin et al,1993) demonstrated that moderate activity burns slightly more fat than an activity such as hard running.

It's a good idea to start with low intensity exercise and build up to higher intensity as it gives better cardio improvements and takes less time to burn the same number of calories.

LOWER YOUR STRESS LEVELS

Training helps to release stress and has a calming effect on the mind and body. Your body has a default position for dealing with danger. It's the stress response to help us deal with emergencies. However, if the stress response is regularly set off, it can cause health problems, if not managed well.

The feeling of having to deal constantly with stress and problems that are out of your control can have long-term and serious consequences such as a heart attack.

Unrealistic expectations can lead to people putting themselves under pressure because they're anxious and afraid of lacking physical, intellectual or emotional strengths and constantly seek approval from those around them.

If you are a perfectionist, you are destined to be unhappy. Don't hide your emotions as they may turn into a powder keg of anger. Learn tolerance and forgiveness, develop listening and assertiveness rather than anger and hostility. However, know when and how to turn on your aggressive self and when to turn it off.

GIVE YOURSELF A TREAT AND AVOID GOING A BIT CRAZY

Avoid going nuts by giving yourself a treat once a week. Some people cannot switch off and become total fitness freaks or martial arts bores. Always talking about how tough they are, how much they can lift and their diet – or putting endless photos of their biceps, abs or dinner on Facebook. Have a day off, take a break, get a massage or eat a nice meal and socialise and enjoy life.

But just don't eat a massive curry, followed by chocolate cake and several pints of lager or a bottle of wine and still think that it's going to help you lose weight and keep fit. Confine your treats within reasonable limits so that it's not all an uphill struggle the next week.

IT'S OK TO BE SELFISH AT THE START

Before you can help anyone you must help yourself. Empowerment must come from within you, your soul and spirit. When barriers are put in your way, knock them down mentally and physically, and with determination and courage.

Only when you feel really confident will you have the strength, confidence and credibility to help others. In the end JKD is really about love and being a happy warrior. It's not about hurting people but helping them towards a better life.

BEING GRATEFUL

Be grateful to those who help you along the way: the creator, your family, friends, instructors, students. You have learned that using a JKD approach is really about being a brave and happy warrior. Standing up for yourself and what you believe in, being assertive rather than angry.

It's about participating and making your life, your community and the world a better place. Even in the face of great enemies, tyrants, bullies and terror.

FINDING MY CONFIDENCE AND HOW TO HANDLE IT

When I first started to learn martial arts I was afraid and beaten down.

But I discovered that as my confidence began to grow, I became less anxious. And as I progressed I found I wasn't afraid of anything.

This was a mistake. I started facing up to everyone. It's easy to become rather cocky, puffed up and arrogant – and this is a trap.

People don't like those who are egotistical and arrogant. I had to learn that dealing with fear or anxiety doesn't have to be like facing a lion head-on. Being quietly confident and having good inner-strength is much better.

ENJOY THE RIDE

It's a funny thing but martial arts training will soon show you that you are not Bruce Lee, Dan Inosanto, Taky Kimura or any great Instructor.

It will dawn on you that you are not that good compared to them and even if you trained hard for the rest of your life you will never catch up on them because they are already too far ahead.

There is always someone much better than you, so all you can do is the best that you can and give your honest effort.

Bruce Lee displayed a dynamic persona that attracted hundreds of thousands of people – myself included – who wanted to be like him. But they soon found out they were not him.

Don't become obsessed with trying to be someone else as it will make you sad and unhappy trying to be a clone of another person. Just be yourself.

A JKD health and wellbeing approach will help you and your loved ones and others to improve their lives and those of the ones that they love and care about. By taking positive action making yourself and others feel better and happier, you will find great satisfaction and true health and wellbeing. Getting mentally prepared for fitness

MAKING A STRONG START

Take a moment and have a think about changing your life for the better. Imagine yourself becoming fitter and stronger and developing more speed and power. Thinking smarter and more positively and transforming your life. All you have to do is take the first step and embrace the changes.

MY FIRST NIGHT AT KARATE

My first night at karate was in Dublin, Ireland, in December 1975. My brother had told me about a good tough club in Parnell Square in the city centre.

I wandered around the square and eventually found a basement. Behind the door were voices and occasional shouting kiai battle cries.

I was anxious and stood at the door for a while before I got the courage to knock and go in. There were about 20 men there all training in front of a black belt, Brian Mc Carthy.

He asked me if I wanted to train and if was healthy and fit enough. That was it, I had started.

The training was warm-ups, push-ups, sit-ups and basic technique for the first hour. Then combinations and partner work, followed by sparring for the next hour. It was hard training but once I got into it I loved it.

ENCOURAGE YOURSELF TO MAKE THE FIRST STEP

THE WILL TO WIN

Imagine yourself winning every time. This will to win is vital and we do this by committing ourselves to challenging training sessions. Training shouldn't be about doing a few exercises and then having a coffee break. If you want to succeed and be mentally tough you have to get active.

This training programme will strengthen your mental will to win. Some of the major factors involved in physical activity are psychological:

- O biological
- O behavioural
- O social
- O cultural
- O environmental
- O and then physical.

A few of the main reasons for joining in activities are enjoyment, self-motivation, social support, education, outcomes. Train often and find a great training partner to work with as it's twice the fun.

NEVER GIVE UP

Life is a battle with our own worst instincts. Having the attitude of never giving up will change your life for the better. It strengthens your mind and body and could literally save your life. Because if attacked on the street, the winner is almost always the one with the most determination. Not the one who is fit, has a six-pack and lovely technique.

This is seen so many areas in life that the one with the strongest mindset and who imposes this on an adversary will constantly win the battle.

Taking responsibility for our actions, thoughts and behaviour in both success and failure is a helpful way to bring about change. Taking action is the most important thing – not just thinking about it, but doing it.

Actions speak louder than words. Learn from failure and don't repeat it. Choose not to feel fear or embarrassment.

SPEAKING IN FRONT OF A CROWD

Public speaking often comes top of the list for people when it comes to fear-inducing and terrifying activities.

When I first had to do this, I was very anxious. But the more I did it, the more I gradually became comfortable with it.

I had to do this during my work, often presenting to a board of directors, and I did it as a martial arts instructor and learned to do so competently, confidently and successfully.

LOOKING AFTER YOURSELF AND OTHERS

Helping yourself before you can help anyone else is a vital task. Empowerment comes from within and no one can give this to you. You need to believe in yourself and have patience.

When barriers are put in your way, confidence gives the ability to knock them down mentally and physically with determination and courage. Only when you are feeling really confident will you have the inner strength, ability and credibility to help others.

Work at being 100% accountable within your personal life, finance, work career, and health and wellbeing. This enables you to take responsibility for your successes and failures. Remember that humans learn more from failure than success, this is how progress has been made in science and technology.

Ultimately, the JKD approach is really about love of humanity and family, and being a happy warrior. However, high fives come at the end of hard training sessions and not as a substitute for it.

You have learned in this chapter that building your confidence and self-esteem is a powerful way to improve your life and circumstances. This in turn gives you more ability to seize opportunities or deal with problems that come your way.

This is an important key connection between having a positive mindset and improving your health and wellbeing.

DRUG TAKING AND COMMUNITY EDUCATION

Young people are more at risk from drug taking. One of the ways I became involved in my social work job was through identifying a really good drug and substance educational project that was working well in a working class area of Dublin, Ireland

I then convinced my then-chief executive to invest tens of thousands of pounds to fund it for several years.

This enabled parents and young people to participate at no cost in the programme. The project trained hundreds of volunteers about the danger of drugs and alcohol misuse they were able to bring this experience back to their families and communities.

At Risk Youth have been helped by our local Clann Eireann Youth Club and outreach team of dedicated youth workers and young peer volunteers, who work directly with vulnerable young people in the area.

APPENDIX

WORKOUTS

"There are not 50 ways of fighting there is only
one, and that's to win."
Mairaux

APPENDIX

THE WORKOUTS

DRILLS

The following activities and drills are taken from JKD arts to provide variety and interest. These can be mixed and matched and chosen to help you to have a great workout. They can be used to add variety and prevent boredom creeping in and killing motivation.

HELPFUL TIPS

These will also be covered with step-by-step instructions in our YouTube videos

Note: Single Direct Attack (SDA) includes individual single jab, cross, hook, uppercut and others.
Attacks By Combination (ABC) includes any two or more techniques such as jab, cross and kick or others.

WEEK 1-3 DRILL COMBINATION

○ jab x 1 min
○ cross x 1 min
○ hook x 1 min
○ jab – cross – hook x 1 min
○ hook kick x 1 min

WEEK 4-7 DRILL COMBINATION

○ jab – cross x 2 min
○ jab – cross – hook x 2 min
○ jab – cross – 2 uppercuts x 2 min
○ jab – cross – 2 uppercuts – 2 knees x 2 min

WEEK 8-12 DRILL COMBINATION

○ jab – cross – hook x 2 min
○ 2 elbows x 2 min
○ 2 knees x 2 min
○ hook kick x 2 min
○ side kick x 2 min
○ footwork and movement x 2 min
○ (add an extra minute to each one for a harder workout)

OPTIONAL DRILLS

For more variety and greater progression, you can include this into your sessions.

DRILL 1

HEAVY BAG BOXING, EACH ARE 2 MINUTE ROUNDS

- O jab
- O cross
- O hook
- O jab

DRILL 2

HEAVY BAG KICKING, EACH ARE 2 MINUTE ROUNDS

- O hook kick
- O side kick
- O straight kick

DRILL 3

THAI BOXING WORKOUT, EACH ARE 2 MINUTE ROUNDS

- O rear leg round kick
- O front leg round kick
- O left and right elbows
- O left and right knees

DRILL 4

SPARRING DRILL

Note: A game like "Tag" with partner, very light contact to partner's shoulder or leg, keep hands up and move in all directions! This is a lighter form of sparring that works on speed and agility. Focus on speed and mobility, maintaining on guard throughout. Don't hit hard.

Sparring game	
Start	1. On guard 2. Tag game 3. Face partner 4. Hands up 5. Chin down 6. Use fast footwork
Technique	7. Hands open 8. Tap partner's leg or shoulder
Close	9. Return to on guard 10. Change partners /roles of attacker and defender

DRILL 5

STRAIGHT BLAST PUNCHING

- ○ punching x 10 seconds x 8 sets
- ○ 20 seconds rest between sets

NOTES ON PROGRESSION

Kickboxing is a great way to add variety and fun to your activities. It builds timing, cardiovascular capacity, and dynamic strength and stamina. This challenges and conditions the body quickly and you should feel a bit puffed.

Begin with basic solo shadow sparring and build to hitting the heavy bag, focus pads, speed bag or top and bottom bag as this adds a fantastic and enjoyable aspect to the workouts.

Start with one or two-minute rounds, building up to five to ten rounds. When you can do this go to three-minute rounds for five rounds or more.

Tip: On day one, take photos on a light background in your underwear of the front, side and back of your body. This will be a visual record of your progress. Do this every week on Friday mornings at the same time and place before breakfast and after going to the toilet. Then make a note of your exact weight.

PULSE RAISER OPTIONS

In gym: Treadmill, rowing machine, static bike, step-up on a box.

Out gym: Skipping, shadow boxing, footwork, heavy bag and focus pads.

RESISTANCE DAY COMPONENTS

Do these three times a week on Monday, Wednesday and Friday.

Component	Description	Benefit
Pulse raise	Activating the body for training and raising the pulse	Your body is ready for the session and reduces risk of injury
Resistance	Gradually increasing the weight lifted will make you stronger	Strength gains and more powerful muscles
Abs and core	Strengthening the core leads to better overall conditioning	A strong body in all ranges of motion
Cooldown	Light mobility exercises and stretching	Reduces soreness and prevents injuries

LIGHT TRAINING DAYS

Do these three times a week on Tuesday, Thursday and Saturday

Component	Description	Benefit
Pulse raise	A light run, yoga or other class of choice	Keep the body active and flexible between hard workouts
Abs and core	Active core exercises	Keeps the body activated and strong
Developmental stretching	Full body stretching strengthens muscles	Gets a better full range of motion in the body
Cooldown	Light mobility exercises and stretching	Reduces soreness and prevents injuries

WEEK 1 TO 3

WEEK 1 TO 3 MONDAYS

PULSE RAISER

Exercise name	Description
Treadmill / shadow boxing	4 mins

DRILLS

Combo	Description
1. Jab	1 min
2. Jab – cross	1 min

RESISTANCE EXERCISES

1. CHEST DROPSETS

Exercise name	Set	% of 1RM	Reps	Rest
Chest press	1-3	60%	10	1 min
	4	20%	10	

2. Back drop sets

Exercise name	Set	% of 1RM	Reps	Rest
Lat pulldown	1	60%	8	1 min
	2	40%	6	1 min
	3	20%	4	1 min
	4	10%	2	

Alternative if no pulldown machine available

Exercise name	Set	Reps	Rest
Pull-ups	1	5	1 min
	2	4	1 min
	3	4	1 min

3. LEGS MUTE SETS

Exercise name	Set	Rep	Tempo	Rest
Leg extension	1-3	Full	10Cx2E	1 min
	4	3/4	AFAP	

4. SHOULDER PRESS PYRAMIDS

Exercise name	Set	% of 1RM	Reps	Rest
Shoulder press	1	60%	4	1 min
	2	40%	8	1 min
	3	30%	10	1 min
	4	20%	12	

5 . BACK SQUAT SUPERSETS

Exercise name	Set	% of 1RM	Reps	Rest
Back squat	1	60%	8	1 min
	2	50%	8	1 min
	3	40%	8	1 min
	4	20%	8	1 min
Alternate leg dumbbell lunges	1-4	BW	AMAP	0

ABDOMINAL AND CORE EXERCISES

Exercise name	Description
Sit ups	10x3 sets
Plank	30 secs x2

COOLDOWN

Exercise name	Description
Treadmill	4 mins
Stretching	10 mins

SELF-EVALUATION AND ADVICE

Self-evaluation and or verbal feedback discussion at the end of each session for a few minutes. Make a note of how you are feeling and any issues.

- Identify any problems or issues and adjust the programme as required.
- Take advice on nutrition for a healthy lifestyle.

WEEK 1 TO 3 TUESDAYS (AD)

PULSE RAISE

Exercise name	Description
Pulse raise	4 min

DRILLS

Combo	Description
1. Jab	1 min
2. Jab-cross	1 min
3. Jab-cross-hook	1 min

ABDOMINAL AND CORE EXERCISES

Exercise name	Description
Sit ups	10x3 sets
Plank	30secs x 2
Push ups	10x3 sets
Squats	10x3 sets

DEVELOPMENTAL STRETCHING

Exercise name	Description
Stretching	10 min

COOLDOWN

Exercise name	Description
Treadmill walk	4 min

WEEK 1 TO 3 WEDNESDAYS (RD)

PULSE RAISE

Exercise name	Description
Treadmill	4 mins

DRILLS

Combo	Description
1. Jab	1 min
2. Jab-cross	1 min

RESISTANCE EXERCISES

1.   CHEST SETS

Exercise name	Set	% of 1RM	Reps	Rest
Bench press	1-3	60%	10	1 min

2. BACK DROP SETS

Exercise name	Set	% of 1RM	Reps	Rest
Lat pulldown	1	60%	8	1 min
	2	50%	8	1 min
	3	40%	8	1 min
	4	20%	8	

3. LEGS MUTE TRAINING

Exercise name	Set	Rep	Tempo	Rest
Leg extension	1-3	Full	10Cx2E	1 min
	4	3/4	AFAP	

4. BACK AND BICEPS SETS

Exercise name	Set	% of 1RM	Reps	Rest
Barbell upright rows	1-3	60%	10	1 min

5 . BACK AND LEGS SUPERSETS

Exercise name	Set	% of 1RM	Reps	Rest
Back squat	1-4	60%	8	1 min
Alternate leg dumbbell lunges	1-4	BW	AMAP	0

ABDOMINAL AND CORE EXERCISES

Exercise name	Description
Sit ups	10x3 sets
Plank	30secs x 3

COOLDOWN

Exercise name	Description
Treadmill walk	4 min
Stretch	10 min

WEEK 1 TO 3 THURSDAYS (RD)

PULSE RAISE

Exercise name	Description
Skipping	4 min

DRILLS

Combo	Description
1. Jab	1 min
2. Cross	1 min
3. Hook	1 min

ABDOMINAL AND CORE EXERCISES

Exercise name	Description
Sit ups	10x3 sets
Push ups	10x3 sets
Bodyweight squats	10x3 sets

DEVELOPMENTAL STRETCHING

Exercise name	Description
Stretching	10 min

COOLDOWN

Exercise name	Description
Treadmill walk	4 min

WEEK 1 TO 3 FRIDAYS (RD)

PULSE RAISE

Exercise name	Description
Treadmill	4 min

DRILLS

Combo	Description
1. Jab-cross	1 min
2. Jab-cross-hook	1 min

RESISTANCE EXERCISES

1. CHEST DROP SETS

Exercise name	Set	% of 1RM	Reps	Rest
Chest press	1-3	60%	10	1 min
	4	40%	10	

2. BACK NOS SETS

Exercise name	Set	% of 1RM	Reps	Rest
Lat pulldown	1	60%	8	1 min
	2	40%	8	1 min
	3	30%	8	1 min
	4	20%	8	

3. LEG MUTE SETS

Exercise name	Set	Rep	Tempo	Rest
Leg extension ((40% 1RM)	1-3	Full	10Cx2E	1 min
	4	3/4	AFAP	

4. SHOULDER PRESS PYRAMIDS

Exercise name	Set	% of 1RM	Reps	Rest
Shoulder press	1	60%	4	1 min
	2	40%	6	1 min
	3	30%	8	1 min
	4	20%	10	1 min

5 . BACK AND LEG SUPERSET

Exercise name	Set	% of 1RM	Reps	Rest
Back squat	1-3	60%	8	1 min
Alternate leg dumbbell lunges	1-4	BW	AMAP	

ABDOMINAL AND CORE EXERCISES

Exercise name	Description
Sit ups	10x3 sets
Leg raises to 45 degrees	10x2 sets
Plank	45secs x 1

COOLDOWN

Exercise name	Description
Treadmill walk	4 min
Stretch	10 min

WEEK 1 TO 3 SATURDAYS (RD)

PULSE RAISE

Exercise name	Description
Treadmill	4 min

DRILLS

Combo	Description
1. Double jab (two jabs)	1 min
2. Jab-cross	1 min
3. Jab-cross-hook	1 min

ABDOMINAL AND CORE EXERCISES

Exercise name	Description
Sit ups	10x3 sets
Thrusters	10x3 sets
Push ups	10x3 sets

DEVELOPMENTAL STRETCHING

Exercise name	Description
Stretching (Note: hold for 15 to 30 seconds)	5 min

COOLDOWN

Exercise name	Description
Treadmill	4 min

WEEK 1 TO 3 SUNDAY (REVIEW)

Mentally note what went well and how you are progressing. Make
sure your log sheets or apps are completed

- O review your self-assessment and notes
- O note your emotional mental feeling of overall wellbeing
- O note physical wellbeing
- O look in the mirror – do you look and feel healthier
- O repeat lifestyle audit
- O what is going well
- O what needs to improve
- O reward yourself for completing first phase

WEEK 4 TO 7

WEEK 4 TO 7 MONDAYS

PULSE RAISER

Exercise name	Description
Treadmill	3 min

DRILLS

Combo	Description
1. Jab-cross-straight kick	2 min
2. Jab-cross-hook-hook kick	2 min
3. Jab-cross-uppercut-2 knee spikes	1 min

RESISTANCE EXERCISES

1. CHEST DROP SETS

Exercise name	Set	% of 1RM	Reps	Rest
Chest press	1-3	60%	10	1 min
	4	20%	10	1 min

2. BACK DROP SETS

Exercise name	Set	% of 1RM	Reps	Rest
Lat pulldown	1	70%	6	1 min
	2	60%	8	1 min
	3	50%	10	1 min
	4	20%	12	1 min

3. LEGS MUTE SETS

Exercise name	Set	Rep	Tempo	Rest
Leg extension (40% of 1 RM)	1-3	Full	10Cx2E	1 min
	4	3/4	AFAP	

4. SHOULDER PRESS PYRAMIDS

Exercise name	Set	% of 1RM	Reps	Rest
Shoulder press	1	70%	4	1 min
	2	50%	8	1 min
	3	40%	12	1 min
	4	20%	16	

5 . BACK SQUAT SUPERSETS

Exercise name	Set	% of 1RM	Reps	Rest
Back squat	1	70%	4	1 min
	2	50%	8	1 min
	3	30%	12	1 min
	4	20%	16	1 min
Alternate leg dumbbell lunges	1-4	BW	AMAP	0

ABDOMINAL AND CORE EXERCISES

Exercise name	Description
Sit ups	10 x 3 sets
Plank	1min x 2

COOLDOWN

Exercise name	Description
Treadmill	4 min
Stretching	10 min

Notes: The treadmill is used to rewarm the body for stretching

SELF-EVALUATION AND ADVICE

Self-evaluation and or verbal feedback discussion at the end of each session for a few minutes. Make a note of how you are feeling and any issues.

- ○ Identify any problems or issues and adjust the programme as required.
- ○ Take advice and seek quality information on nutrition for a healthy lifestyle.

WEEK 4 TO 7 TUESDAY

PULSE RAISER

Exercise name	Description
Treadmill	4 min

DRILLS

Combo	Description
1. Jab-cross-hook kick	1 min
2. Jab-cross-side kick	1 min
3. Jab-cross-hook	1 min
4. Jab-cross-hook-2 uppercuts (using both hands)	1 min

ABDOMINAL AND CORE EXERCISES

Exercise name	Description
Sit ups	10 x 3 sets
Plank	45secs x 3
Push ups	10 x 3 sets
Squats	10 x 3 sets

DEVELOPMENTAL STRETCHING

Exercise name	Description
Stretching	10 min

COOLDOWN

Exercise name	Description
Treadmill walk	4 min

WEEK 3 TO 7 WEDNESDAY (RD)

PULSE RAISER

Exercise name	Description
Treadmill	4 min

DRILLS

Combo	Description
1. Jab-cross-hook-2 knees	1 min
2. Jab-cross-hook kick	1 min
3. Jab-cross-hook-2 horizontal elbows	1 min

RESISTANCE EXERCISES

1. CHEST AND BACK

Exercise name	Set	% of 1RM	Reps	Rest
Bench Chest Press	123	60%	10	1 min

2. BACK DROPSETS

Exercise name	Set	% of 1RM	Reps	Rest
Lat Pulldown	1	80%	8	1 min
	2	60%	8	1 min
	3	40%	8	1 min
	4	20%	8	1 min

3. LEGS SET

Exercise name	Set	Rep	Tempo	Rest
Leg extension	1	Full	10Cx2E	1 min
	2-4	3/4		1 min

4. BACK AND BICEPS

Exercise name	Set	% of 1RM	Reps	Rest
Upright rows	1-3	60%	10	1 min

5. Legs and back supersets

Exercise name	Set	% of 1RM	Reps	Rest
Back squat	1-4	60%	8	1 min
Alternate leg dumbbell lunges	1-4	BW	AMAP	1 min

ABDOMINAL AND CORE EXERCISES

Exercise name	Description
Sit ups	10x3 sets
Plank	45secs x 3

COOLDOWN

Exercise name	Description
Treadmill walk	4 min
Stretch	10 min

Note: Stretching properly increases the range of motion around a joint. ROM

WEEK 3 TO 7 THURSDAY (AD)

PULSE RAISE

Exercise name	Description
Treadmill	4 min

DRILLS

Combo	Description
1. Jab-cross-hook	1 min
2. Jab-cross-hook-2 elbows	30 secs
3. Jab-cross-hook-hook kick	1 min
4. Jab-cross-2 elbows-2 knees	30 secs

ABDOMINAL AND CORE EXERCISES

Exercise name	Description
Sit ups	10x3 sets
Push ups	10x3 sets
Bodyweight squats	10x3 sets

DEVELOPMENTAL STRETCHING

Exercise name	Description
Stretching	10 min

COOLDOWN

Exercise name	Description
Treadmill	4 min

WEEK 3 TO 7 FRIDAYS

PULSE RAISE

Exercise name	Description
Treadmill	4 min

DRILLS

Combo	Description
1. Jab-cross-hook	1 min
2. Jab-cross-2 uppercuts	1min
3. Jab-cross-2 uppercuts-2 knees	1 min

RESISTANCE EXERCISES

1. CHEST DROP SETS

Exercise name	Set	% of 1RM	Reps	Rest
Chest press	1-3	60%	10	1 min
	4	40%	10	1 min

2. BACK NOS TRAINING

Exercise name	Set	% of 1RM	Reps	Rest
Lat pulldown	1	80%	8	1 min
	2	60%	8	1 min
	3	40%	8	1 min
	4	20%	8	1.min

3. LEGS MUTE SET

Exercise name	Set	Rep	Tempo	Rest
Leg extension (40% of 1 RM)	1	Full	10Cx2E	1 min
	4	3/4	AFAP	1 min

4. SHOULDER PRESS PYRAMIDS

Exercise name	Set	% of 1RM	Reps	Rest
Shoulder press	1	70%	4	1 min
	2	50%	6	1 min
	3	30%	8	1 min
	4	20%	10	1 min

5 . BACK AND LEG SUPERSET

Exercise name	Set	% of 1RM	Reps	Rest
Back squat	1	60%	8	1 min
	2	60%	8	1 min
	3	60%	8	1 min
	4	60%	8	1 min
Alternate leg dumbbell lunges	1-4	BW	AMAP	0

ABDOMINAL AND CORE EXERCISES

Exercise name	Description
Sit ups	10x3
Leg raises	10x3
Plank (45 secs)	2 sets

Note: For leg raises, go up to 45 degrees and on lowering phase don't let the heels touch the floor, keep knees slightly bent, hands supporting the low back.

COOLDOWN

Exercise name	Description
Treadmill walk	4 min
Stretch	10 min

WEEK 3 TO 7 SATURDAY

PULSE RAISE

Exercise name	Description
Treadmill	4 min
Stretch	10 min

DRILLS

Combo	Description
1. Jab-cross	1 min
2. Jab-cross-hook	1 min
3. Jab-cross-hook-2 uppercuts	1 min
4. Jab-cross-hook-side kick	30 secs

ABDOMINAL AND CORE EXERCISES

Exercise name	Description
Sit ups	10x4 sets
Thrusters	10x4 sets
Push ups	10x4 sets

DEVELOPMENTAL STRETCHING

Exercise name	Description
Stretching	5 mins

COOLDOWN

Exercise name	Description
Treadmill	4 mins

WEEK 4 TO 6 SUNDAY (REVIEW)

- mental review – what went well, progress, fill in log sheets
- review your self-assessment or notes from trainer
- overall wellbeing: how you are feeling emotionally and physically?
- look in the mirror – do you look healthier
- step on the scales and check your weight
- take photos in underwear and review the photos taken at the beginning of week one. photo of front and side and back of the body

WEEK 7 SUNDAY (REVIEW)

This is an opportunity to take a look back at the progress that you have made up to week 7. Take time to reflect on how you felt at the beginning and how you are feeling now.

Think about what is going well regarding your nutrition, eating patterns, activities, sleep pattern. How do you feel emotionally and physically compared to when you started? Look at your training diary and note progress and challenges that you have met so far. Think about and reflect upon your journey to date, how far you have come and the adventures still ahead.

- ○ note what you have achieved and is going well
- ○ what still needs to improve
- ○ reward yourself and give yourself a pat on the back for your achievements

WEEK 8 TO 12

WEEK 8 TO 12 MONDAYS

PULSE RAISER

Exercise name	Description
Treadmill	4 mins

DRILLS

Combo	Description
1. Hook kick-cross-hook- cross	1 min
2. Side kick-cross-2 elbows	30 secs
3. Sweep kick-back fist	1 min
4. Jab-cross-hook-2 uppercuts-2 knees	30 secs

RESISTANCE EXERCISES

1. CHEST DROPSETS

Exercise name	Set	% of 1RM	Reps	Rest
Chest press	1-3	60%	10	1 min
	4	20%	10	1 min

2. BACK DROPSETS

Exercise name	Set	% of 1RM	Reps	Rest
Lat pulldown	1	70%	6	1 min
	2	60%	8	1 min
	3	40%	10	1 min
	4	20%	14	1 min

3. LEGS MUTE

Exercise name	Set	Rep	Tempo	Rest
Leg extension	1	Full	10Cx2E	1 min
	2	Full	10Cx2E	1 min
	3	Full	10Cx2E	1 min
	4	3/4	AFAP	1 min

Note: 10 seconds upward motion and 2 seconds downward motion. Ensure the pad is on the lower leg not the feet..

4. SHOULDER PRESS PYRAMIDS

Exercise name	Set	% of 1RM	Reps	Rest
Shoulder press	1	70%	4	1 min
	2	60%	8	1 min
	3	40%	12	1 min
	4	20%	16	1 min

5 . BACK SQUAT SUPERSETS

Exercise name	Set	% of 1RM	Reps	Rest
Back squat	1	80%	8	1 min
	2	60%	8	1 min
	3	40%	8	1 min
	4	20%	8	1 min
Alternate leg dumbbell lunges	1	BW	20	0
	2	BW	20	0
	3	BW	20	0
	4	BW	20	0

ABDOMINAL AND CORE EXERCISES

Exercise name	Description
Sit ups	10 x 3 sets
Plank	1min x 3 sets

Note: For sit ups, raise the shoulders just off the floor

COOLDOWN

Exercise name	Description
Treadmill	4 mins
Stretching	10 min

Notes: for Sit ups raise the shoulders just off the floor

WEEK 8 TO 12 TUESDAY

PULSE RAISER

	Description
Treadmill	4 min

DRILLS

	Description
1 – Two hook kicks (front and rear leg)	1 min
2 – Two sidekicks (front and rear leg)	30 secs
3 – Two straight kicks (front and rear leg)	1 min
4 – Double knees (left and right)	30 secs
5 – Double elbows (left and right)	1 min

ABDOMINAL AND CORE EXERCISES

	Description
Sit ups	10 x 4 sets
Plank (60 secs)	2 sets
Push ups	10 x 4 sets
Squats	10 x 4 sets

COOLDOWN

	Description
Treadmill	4 min
Static bike	
Rowing machine	

DEVELOPMENTAL STRETCHING

	Description
Stretching	10 min

WEEK 8 TO 12 WEDNESDAY

PULSE RAISER

Exercise name	Description
Treadmill	4 min

DRILLS

Combo	Description
1. Back kick	1 min
2. Side kick-finger jab	30 secs
3. Hook kick-back fist	1 min
4. Jab-cross-hook-2 uppercuts-2 knees	30 secs

RESISTANCE EXERCISES

1. CHEST

Exercise name	Set	% of 1RM	Reps	Rest
Bench Chest Press	1-3	80%	8	1 min

2. BACK DROPSETS

Exercise name	Set	% of 1RM	Reps	Rest
Lat pulldown	1	70%	8	1 min
	2	60%	8	
	3	40%	8	
	4	20%	8	

3. LEGS

Exercise name	Set	Rep	Tempo	Rest
Leg extension	1	Full	10Cx2E	1 min

4. BICEPS AND FOREARMS TYPE

Exercise name	Set	% of 1RM	Reps	Rest
Bicep curls	1-3	60%	10	1 min

5. BACK AND LEGS AND SUPERSETS

Exercise name	Set	% of 1RM	Reps	Rest
Back squat	1-3	70%	8	0
Alternate leg dumbbell lunges	1-4	BW	AMAP	1 min

ABDOMINAL AND CORE EXERCISES

Exercise name	Description
Full sit ups	10 x 3 sets
Plank	1min x 3 sets

COOLDOWN

Exercise name	Description
Treadmill walk	4 min
Stretch	10 min

WEEK 8 TO 12 THURSDAY

PULSE RAISER

Exercise name	Description
Treadmill	4 min

DRILLS

Combo	Description
1. Double jab-2 palm smashes	1 min
2. Jab-cross-straight kick	30 secs
3. Jab-cross-hook-2 horizontal elbows-2 knees	1 min
4. Jab-cross-hook-2 downward elbows	45 secs
5. Straight blast x 5 seconds burst	5 sets

ABDOMINAL AND CORE EXERCISES

Exercise name	Description
Sit ups	10x4 sets
Push ups	10x4 sets
Bodyweight squats	10x5 sets

DEVELOPMENTAL STRETCHING

Exercise name	Description
All stretches	10 min

COOLDOWN

Exercise name	Description
Treadmill	4 min

WEEK 8 TO 12 FRIDAY

PULSE RAISER

Exercise name	Description
Treadmill	4 min

DRILLS

Combo	Description
1. Jab-cross-hook-2 uppercuts	1 min
2. Hook kick-cross-jab-cross	30 secs
3. Side kick-finger jab	45 secs
4. Jab-2 diagonal elbows-lead knee	30 secs
5. Jab-2 horizontal elbows-2 knees	1 min

RESISTANCE EXERCISES

1. CHEST DROP SETS

Exercise name	Set	% of 1RM	Reps	Rest
Chest press	1-3	70%	8	1 min
	4	40%	10	1 min

2. BACK NOS TRAINING

Exercise name	Set	% of 1RM	Reps	Rest
Lat pulldown	1	70%	8	1 min
	2	60%	8	1 min
	3	40%	8	1 min
	4	20%	8	1 min

3. LEG MUTE TRAINING

Exercise name	Set	Rep	Tempo	Rest
Leg extension (70% of 1 RM)	1	Full	10Cx2E	1 min
	2			1 min
	3			1 min
	4	3/4	fast	1 min

4. SHOULDER PRESS PYRAMIDS

Exercise name	Set	% of 1RM	Reps	Rest
Shoulder press	1	70%	4	1 min
	2	60%	6	1 min
	3	40%	8	1 min
	4	20%	10	1 min

5. BACK AND LEG SUPERSET

Exercise name	Set	% of 1RM	Reps	Rest
Back squat	1	70%	8	1 min
	2	70%	8	1 min
	3	70%	8	1 min
	4	70%	8	1 min
Alternate leg dumbbell lunges	1-4	BW	AMAP	0

ABDOMINAL AND CORE EXERCISES

Exercise name	Description
Sit ups	10 x 4 sets
Leg raises	10 x 4 sets
Pull ups	6 x 3 sets

COOLDOWN

Exercise name	Description
Treadmill walk	4 min
Stretch	10 min

WEEK 8 TO 12 SATURDAY

PULSE RAISER

Exercise name	Description
Treadmill	4 min

DRILLS

Combo	Description
1. Jab	1 min
2. Jab-cross	30 secs
3. Jab-cross-hook	1 min
4. Cross-hook-cross	30 secs
5. Front leg hook kick-cross-2 knees	1 min

ABDOMINAL AND CORE EXERCISES

Exercise name	Description
Sit ups	10x5 sets
Thrusters	10x5 sets
Push ups	10x5 sets

DEVELOPMENTAL STRETCHING

Exercise name	Description
Stretching	10 min

COOLDOWN

Exercise name	Description
Treadmill walk	4 min

WEEK 8 TO 12 SUNDAY (REVIEW)

A full evaluation of what went well and how you have progressed. Make sure log sheets are filled in and complete a review of the full 12-week programme:

- take photos and compare the ones that were taken during the 12 weeks
- review your self-assessment and notes from trainer if required
- review your overall wellbeing physical and emotional state
- how do you feel inside
- do look and feel stronger
- how is your cardiovascular conditioning
- how is your nutrition
- note your flexibility
- how are your eating and drinking patterns
- are you getting enough sleep
- look in the mirror – do you look healthier
- redo lifestyle audit
- how is your social life
- what is going well
- what needs to improve

Congratulations and well done – reward yourself for completing the 12-week programme.

Have a celebration (don't overdo it) and then start the next phase.

Maintain your progress and keep moving forward by setting your new goals.

REFERENCES AND RECOMMENDED READING

I have provided a list of books and resources which I have found helpful if you would like to read more on the subject.

My advice is to read the books written by Bruce Lee first, all of which are available on Amazon. I would point you towards "Basic Training" which contains excellent advice on getting it right from the start.

Many people have tried to interpret what Bruce said, but go to the source and read it for yourself. Remember that he changed his mind about some things over the course of weeks, months and years. However, the basic core of his thinking about martial arts did not change very much at all as it was based on science, physics, research and development.

But, of course, collect as many books as you wish if you have the money and take from them what you want.

Commentaries on the Martial Way is also a very good resource with all the essentials in one book.

Chapter 1

Little, J *Bruce Lee's Commentaries on the Martial Way*: Tuttle Co Inc, Boston, (1997)

Bishop, J *Bruce Lee: Dynamic Becoming*, 1st edn., Texas: Promethean Press, (2010)

Little J. *Bruce Lee Artist of Life*: Tuttle Publishing USA, (1999)

Chapter 2

Little, J *The Warrior Within: The Philosophies of Bruce Lee*, 1st edn., New York: Mc Graw-Hill Education, (1996)

Lee B. *Tao of Jeet Kune Do*: Tuttle Publishing, VT, (1975)

Inosanto,D *Absorb what is Useful* : Los Angeles Know Now Publishing Co, (1982)

Lee B and Uyehara M. *Bruce Lee's Fighting Method Basic Training*: OHara Publications, Los Angeles, (1977)

Chapter 3

Inosanto,D *Absorb what is Useful* : Los Angeles Know Now Publishing Co, (1982)

Lee B and Uyehara M. *Bruce Lee's Fighting Method Basic Training*: OHara Publications, Los Angeles, (1997)

Lee, B *Tao of Jeet Kune Do*: Tuttle Publishing, VT, 1975

Chapter 4

Davis M. Jun Fan Jeet Kune Do Scientific Streetfighting: HnL Publishing New York, (1999)

Rooney M. *Ultimate Warrior Workouts*: New York Harper, (2010)

Personal Training Manual Central YMCA Qualifications London:2013

www. cyq. org. uk

Consterdine P. *Fit to Fight*: Leeds, Protection Publications, (1996)

Fairbairn W E. *Get Tough*: Paladin Press Boulder Colorado,(1979)

Mc Cann K. *Combatives for Street Survival*: Black Belt Books OHara Publications Los Angeles, (2009)

De Beker G. *The Gift of Fear*. Dell Publishing, New York, (1998)

Miller, R *Facing violence: preparing for the unexpected*, USA: YMAA, (2011)

MacYoung, M *Cheap shots, ambushes and other lessons*, USA: Paladin Press, (1989)

Workouts

Department of Health (2004) *At Least 5 a Week: Evidence on the impact of physical activity and its relationship to health*, London: DoH, (2004)

Ratamess, N *ACSM's Foundations of Strength Training and Conditioning (American College of Sports Med)*, Indianapolis: Lippincott Williams and Wilkins, (2011)

Personal Training Manual Central *YMCA Qualifications* London, (2013)

Peters, D *Total Health*, London: Marshall Publishing. (1998)

Goodsell, A *Your Personal Trainer*, London: Boxtree Limited, (1994)

Lombardi,V *Run to Win*, USA: St Martin's Griffin, (2002)

Mac Young , M for detailed advice see
www.nononsesenceselfdefence.com

Bibliography

Mushashi, M *Book of Five Rings*: New York Overlord Press, (1974)

Hartsell, L *Jeet Kune Do Entering to Trapping to Grappling*: Unique Publications, Burbank, (1984)

O'Morain P. *Mindfulness on the Go*, London: Yellow Kite, Hodder and Stoughton, (2014)

THANKS FOR READING

You have learned about how following a JKD approach can assist you to have a better quality of life and improve your health and wellbeing. By taking control of your destiny you can shape it, avoid pipe dreams and hoping that your luck will change for the better, because it won't.

Looking after your physical health and wellbeing leads to building your resilience and inner emotional strength.

By following the physical training outlined in the book this will help you to build your body to be strong and fit.

Learn from mistakes because that is how humanity has made most advances in medicine, science, technology and martial arts.

Best wishes to you in your life,

Martin O'Neill

2017

RESOURCES

You can download all the workouts in the annex from the website:
www.jkdireland.com/book-resources

You can view the demonstration videos on my website:
www.jkdireland.com/demo-videos.html

The gym exercise demonstration videos are available here:
www.bodybuilding.com

KEEP IN TOUCH

TELL ME YOUR STORY

Keep in touch and tell me your JKD story. I'd love to hear from you. You can drop me an email at: info@jkdireland.com.

JOIN MY FACEBOOK PAGE

Join my Facebook page for more information on JKD and self-protection.
www.facebook.com/JKDIreland/

WORK WITH ME

If you would like me to help you with your JKD training or your fitness programme, you can find out more here:

www.jkdireland.com/work-with-me

www.ingramcontent.com/pod-product-compliance
Lightning Source LLC
Chambersburg PA
CBHW071525040426
42452CB00008B/894